MORE
THAN
ONE

MORE
THAN
ONE

TERRI A. CLARK, M.D.

THOMAS NELSON PUBLISHERS
Nashville

Published in Nashville, Tennessee, by Oliver-Nelson Books, a division of Thomas Nelson, Inc., Publishers, and distributed in Canada by Word Communications, Ltd., Richmond, British Columbia, and in the United Kingdom by Word (UK), Ltd., Milton Keynes, England.

The Bible version used in this publication is THE NEW KING JAMES VERSION. Copyright © 1979, 1980, 1982, Thomas Nelson, Inc., Publishers.

The persons described in this book are clinical composites and do not represent specific persons. Names, descriptions, and events have been fictionalized to protect privacy.

Printed in the United States of America.

Library of Congress Cataloging-in-Publication Data

Clark, Terri A., 1955–
    More than one / Terri A. Clark.
        p.   cm.
    Includes bibliographical references.
    ISBN 0-8407-9140-2
    1. Multiple personality.   I. Title.
RC569.5.M8C53   1993
616.85'236—dc20   93-4480
                                                              CIP

1 2 3 4 5 6 — 98 97 96 95 94 93

To
The Almighty and loving Father
and His Son Jesus Christ whose body we compose,
who lives and works through us and in us.

To
My treasured patients
who have been my teachers.

To
Those who have loved me and strengthened me
with their love.

CONTENTS

Resources

IN GRATITUDE

Thank you to all the patients who shared their lives with me. I am a better human being for having known you. You have enriched my life.

Thanks to my staff who have been there for me when I needed them most. Jeanne Sims, Linda Johnson, Cathy Thibodeau, and Stacy Lombard, I couldn't have done this without your help, prayers, and support.

Thanks to Erin Graffy whose talent and hard work have been invaluable in the telling of these precious stories and the writing of this book.

MORE
THAN
ONE

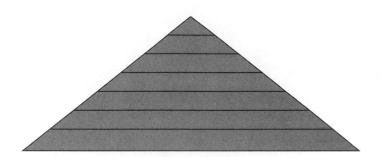

Section 1

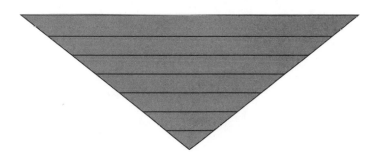

UNCOVERING

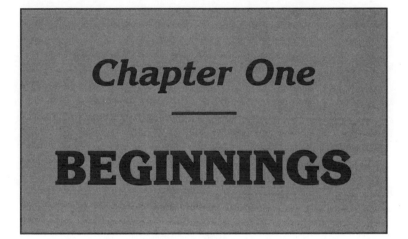

Chapter One

BEGINNINGS

THE NIGHT SHIFT

It was in the middle of the night when I met my first patient with multiple personality disorder. I was the intern in the psychiatric emergency room at Harbor General Hospital in Torrance, California. And I had no idea that on that night my view of people would change dramatically. I would come to see deeper pain and more drastic measures to survive than I ever imagined possible.

About two o'clock in the morning, a petite woman was brought into the psychiatric emergency ward. She is not a vague memory; her imprint is fixed distinctly in my mind. She was in her mid-twenties, with brownish blond hair lightly curled around a pixieish face. She had on a nice pair of dark blue jeans, a teal green T-shirt, a light blue windbreaker, and low-heeled black pumps. There was nothing abnormally remarkable about her appearance.

She was escorted to the nurse on duty at the front desk by two other people. They were part of a suicide precaution procedure because the young woman was bent on self-destruction. It would be my job to determine the severity of her problem and evaluate the likelihood of her killing herself.

Although it was a county hospital, it served some fairly affluent communities—from Malibu through Palos Verdes to Long Beach. Many of our night emergencies were suicidal clients. The patient appeared to be typical of an upper-middle-class female with suicidal ideations.

The nurse at the desk threw me a sideward glance and cleared her throat, "Is your friend here suicidal, or is she feeling maybe a little depressed . . . because of the weather?" she asked dryly.

> *"One of my alter personalities is extremely depressed. She is the one who is suicidal—she just needs to talk to someone, and then she'll be all right."*

The young woman bit her lip. "Well, I . . . yes, um, *I* am seeking help." She took a breath, and then in an attempt to maintain a calm and controlled voice, she said, "I am a multiple—I am a patient undergoing treatment for multiple personality disorder. My psychiatrist is out of town on vacation at the moment, and one of my alter personalities is extremely depressed. *She* is the one who is suicidal—she just needs to talk to someone, and then she'll be all right."

I quickly looked down at the desk to feign finding my notebook and pen. My first reaction was, "I don't think that multiple personality disorder exists." It was hard enough to be an intern and deal with what I *did* know. Multiple personality? It was a bit out of my league. It certainly wasn't something we had discussed much in medical school. I had read *Sybil* and even seen the TV movie about the famous multiple personality, but they were sensationalized and separating truth from fiction was hard. I knew that even though my academic training in the area was weak, I could at least show her that I cared and treat her with the respect she deserved.

The young woman was clearly feeling panicky. Lorinda had a detached matter-of-fact way of describing herself. I had the uncanny feeling I was talking with another clinician rather than a suicidal patient. However nervous she appeared, Lorinda really did seem to know and understand everything about her crisis situation. The question that continued to surface but remained unspoken by me was, "Is this for real?"

"I don't need to be hospitalized. There is no reason to lock anyone up or to keep us as an inpatient. We'll all be fine if someone could just talk to Anne. [Anne was the alter personality who was supposedly suicidal.] We have been in therapy as a multiple for two and a half years, and our regular psychiatrist is in Colorado right now, which is why we are here tonight.

"Anne is depressed because she received a call from her mother—that always makes her depressed. But the mother was really giving her a bad time, and Anne is going over the deep end about it. She feels she can never please her mother. Anne is our birth personality, but I am the one who is usually in charge," Lorinda continued.

"If someone could hear Anne out, it would really relieve her anxieties, and we will all be able to breathe easier. We've had to hide the razor blades because she's been wanting to slit her wrists. We are not dangerous, nor is Anne, but she does need a therapist to talk to right now."

> *The whole time I was taking down her history, my mind was vacillating between treating it as a serious psychiatric problem and writing it off as the incredible imagination of a young woman.*

The whole time I was taking down her history, my mind was vacillating between treating it as a serious psychiatric problem and writing it off as the incredible imagination of a young woman who had regressed to an infantile state of make-believe. Lorinda was straightforwardly knowledgeable—I could believe her on that basis. She was completely lucid, albeit bizarre. I could tell from her explanation of the situation that someone inside her needed help; at least she believed someone did. I had no choice but to treat the beliefs as if they were real.

"Please don't give me medicine," she added quickly, almost as though she had read my thoughts. "Medicine absolutely will not help us—it will only make the splitting worse and make the child alters sick."

I wanted to dismiss the whole thing. After all, many of the mentally ill patients I had seen would make up fantastic stories, or they would have delusions about themselves. Lorinda was different, however. There was something very real and honest about the way she presented everything. I felt that she was fighting for her life in her efforts to get me to listen to her. She seemed desperate to persuade me, and I had to admit she was convincing.

The name of a psychologist who had first worked with Lorinda was given to me. Although I first hesitated to call somcone at such an early hour of the morning, I needed to corroborate what she said. I made contact with her psychologist, and he was able to confirm Lorinda's story in every single aspect, which fascinated me further. I wanted to know more, but I was too embarrassed to ask. Even formulating questions to *think* of asking him felt too awkward for me because they would show how little I knew about the subject.

UNTRAINED AND SKEPTICAL

I was embarrassed that the professional seemed to know so much and accept the problem as a real disorder while I knew so little and was skeptical about what I was witnessing. When I was in medical school, multiple personality disorder was not officially classified as a mental disorder. My entire medical training included no face-to-face contact with multiples and very little information. I could remember perhaps three passing comments about multiple personality disorder from my professors, and they were of a spurious nature. The disorder was placed in the same category as UFOs—things that were highly controversial and that laypeople talked about and desperately believed in, but certainly not rational MDs.

Thus, my very first patient with multiple personality disorder was, in a sense, my very first teacher. Although I never saw Lorinda again, that night was to be the first episode in my clinical experience and the beginning of my relationship with persons with multiple personality disorder. The journey of understanding has been a long one with many breakthroughs and disappointments. But it has been a wonderful journey that has included some incredible people who have made my life more meaningful.

The beginning of my journey was like that of many others in the mental health profession. Ignorance and naiveté are common throughout the medical and mental health field. Although the disorder is increasingly better known, far too many mental health professionals do not believe multiple personality disorder exists. Even those who do, however, believe the condition is so rare that they don't believe it when they see it—in fact, far too many have never properly diagnosed the multiple patients who *have* come into their offices. Patients with multiple personality disorder have usually been in therapy with several professionals for five

> *Although the disorder is increasingly better known, far too many mental health professionals do not believe multiple personality disorder exists.*

to six years before a correct diagnosis is finally made.

Lorinda was one of those rare persons with the disorder who had been correctly diagnosed. Furthermore, she must have been in capable hands because she was familiar enough with her disorder to be able to intelligently describe and explain it to others. I suspect she is well on the way to integrating the separate identities into a whole person.

This disorder has affected me deeply on a personal level. What I once feared, I am drawn to. What I avoided, I now seek out to treat. I am drawn to both the psychological and the spiritual aspects of the disorder. As both a medical doctor and a Christian, I am moved by these patients, their stories, and their perseverence toward the help they need.

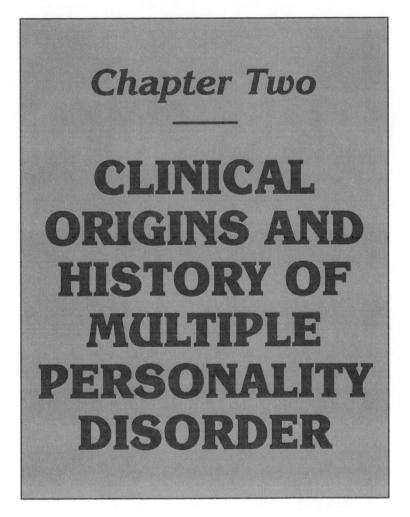

Chapter Two

CLINICAL ORIGINS AND HISTORY OF MULTIPLE PERSONALITY DISORDER

Shortly after my encounter with Lorinda, I began my own research to discover the answers to the following questions: How was multiple personality disorder first discovered? What is the disorder all about anyway? Who could I consult to find out more information? My medical reference books had little about the disorder. How could I possibly learn about this baffling disorder that fellow professionals, textbooks, and my training had almost completely ignored?

PUBLIC AWARENESS

As I stated earlier, like most of the medical profession (as well as the rest of the world), the very first time I heard about multiple personality disorder was through the popular press.

During the late 1950s, *The Three Faces of Eve,* as recounted by two psychiatrists, introduced the world to the concept of multiple personalities.[1] The true story told of the triple personalities of a timid southern housewife, Eve White. Later a movie starring Academy Award-winning actress Joanne Woodward brought the story to the silver screen and out into the public eye. The public was fascinated with the idea of three distinct personalities in one body. Eve the housewife was an almost mousy woman. Eve Black was almost the complete opposite—a gregarious, flamboyant personality who loved to sing and dance at nightclubs. Jane was the stable, articulate woman who was thoughtful, responsible, and confident.

> *Sybil's story made "multiple personalities" a household phrase.*

Barely fifteen years later, the chronicle of *Sybil* made the best-seller list. Another factual account, *Sybil* was based on the story of how child abuse can affect a bright, creative young child. Her mother tortured her daughter from the time Sybil was a toddler of two. Sybil's analyst, Cornelia Wilbur, uncovered seventeen personalities that haunted and protected Sybil's fragile life. The personalities ranged from a young child to a teenage boy named Sid to a sophisticated art connoisseur. As was the case with Eve's story, Sybil's was adapted as a movie, starring yet another Hollywood favorite, Sally Field.

While Eve's story was first responsible for bringing the concept of multiple personalities into the public awareness, Sybil's story made "multiple personalities" a household phrase.

PUBLIC INTEREST

During the eighties and now into the nineties, I have noticed the concept of multiple personality disorder getting far more attention and public discussion. The talk shows have had a field day with the subject. To the astonishment and often the disbelief of the studio audiences, Geraldo Rivera, Oprah Winfrey, and Phil Donahue have featured people with multiple personalities on their shows. As the audience view one personality in one segment and then meet another personality after a commercial break, their skepticism has been quite evident from their questions. Most are cynical; some even mock people with MPD and tell them to grow up.

On the one hand, it is good to see that people are increasingly familiar with the disorder. On the other hand, there is a void of solid, balanced information. As a result, people with multiple personalities are often treated as less-than-human mental oddities.

CLINICAL HISTORY OF MULTIPLE PERSONALITY DISORDER

After meeting with Lorinda, I went into my research mode to get a better understanding of the disorder. I delved into medical reference books and gathered anything I could find on the subject from the medical library. With so many differing opinions on MPD, it wasn't easy developing a balanced understanding of the disorder. And some of the information was surprising.

The first surprise was that the disorder was first noted more than two hundred years ago (so much for the crit-

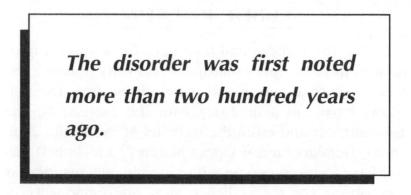

> *The disorder was first noted more than two hundred years ago.*

ics who have dismissed multiple personality disorder as a "new" psychiatric invention!). The earliest reference I could find about the subject was attributed to a German physician named Eberhardt Gmelin in the late eighteenth century. He reported on the interesting case of a female patient and described her as having an "exchanged personality." The young woman had a "French" personality—yet she was a German aristocrat. Her alternate personality was not only fluent in French but also maintained the customs and mannerisms of the French!

I found that other cases throughout the nineteenth century were reported from time to time in the United States, Great Britain, France, and Germany. Those cases were not very detailed and, of course, were written from the perspective of mental health professionals who were practicing in the infancy of a complicated field.

Nonetheless, I was intrigued to see that the disorder was observed so early, and that it was not limited to a few cases observed by only a few doctors.

Right after the turn of the century, in 1905, Dr. Morton Prince wrote a book about multiple personality disorder. His famous case study of Christine "Sally" Beauchamp, a woman with three personalities, was written up in *The Dissociation of a Personality*. This book is still a classic on the subject and was reprinted in 1978.

With Dr. Prince's work as a foundation, information should have continued to add insight to the disorder. But that was not to be. Sigmund Freud repudiated the disorder. His dismissal of multiple personality as a disorder resulted in the topic being dropped from any credible mental health discussions. Since that time, the disorder has been *over*looked, *under*identified, and mostly *mis*diagnosed as either schizophrenia or psychosis.

SCOPE OF THE DISORDER

The number of cases of multiple personality disorder has skyrocketed in the last ten years. Less than twenty years ago, only a hundred cases were reported in America. Today, estimates are that between three to five thousand patients with multiple personality disorder are being treated.[2] This phenomenal increase in cases of multiple personality disorder has left some skeptics with the impression that it is an "in" or "fad" mental illness, which adds to the prevalent distrust of the diagnosis.

DEVELOPMENT OF THE DIAGNOSIS

It is tempting and quite popular to criticize Freud for repressing discussion of multiple personality disorder and to accuse those in mental health for the past eighty years of being in denial about the disorder. That isn't entirely fair because several developments since 1940 have allowed multiple personality disorder to resurface and to finally gain validity. The first development happened after World War II. During the war, hypnosis was used for mind control—for eliciting information from prisoners of war or for brainwashing. The practice awakened an interest in hypnosis for peaceful purposes after the war.

In the field of mental health, hypnosis became a tool for uncovering traumatic incidents in early childhood. As it turned out, the hypnotists discovered two important facts about those with MPD. First of all, those with multiple personality disorder were very easy to hypnotize, making them good candidates for research. As researchers studied them under hypnotic trance, the second major discovery was that almost everyone with multiple personality disorder had been a victim of severe child abuse.

Freud dismissed not only multiple personality disorder but also the concepts of incest and child abuse. The dismissals kept multiple personality disorder submerged, unidentified, and untreated. However, when the liberated 1960s and 1970s pulled many previously taboo subjects out of the closet, the issues of child abuse and incest came to the fore. As they came into awareness, they brought along with them the growing recognition that MPD was something real. When research piled up, the connection between MPD and abuse became evident. Researchers also became aware that the abuse experienced by people with MPD was often torturous in nature.

RECOGNITION OF DIAGNOSIS

Finally, in 1980, the psychiatric community officially recognized multiple personality disorder as an accepted diagnosis. That was the year multiple personality disorder was first listed in the *Diagnostic and Statistical Manual of Mental Disorders.* This book is the reference manual used by the mental health community to diagnose psychiatric problems. If doctors observe certain symptoms and behavior, they can go to the manual and substantiate the diagnosis so as to select the preferred method of treatment. It is the most commonly used handbook in the field of mental health.

Prior to 1980, a mental health professional was not able to find any acceptable diagnosis to exactly match what was showing up in clinics and hospitals. Doctors tried to squeeze their MPD patients into "acceptable" syndromes and labeled them with disorders such as schizophrenia, borderline personality disorder, or mild psychosis that have common symptoms. Once multiple personality disorder "made the book" and became a legitimate psychiatric disorder, professionals could make a correct diagnosis that could lead to proper treatment, but few realized how difficult that treatment would be.

PREVALENCE

Estimates have been given of three to five thousand patients with multiple personality disorder *in treatment.* Many other people with the disorder may not have been properly diagnosed, and still others have never sought help.

Because the psychiatric community has only recently begun to treat and gather information about multiple personality disorder, any statistics released to date should be considered far from conclusive. But these early numbers reveal that it is not a rare disorder limited to a few hundred people. Some practices are overwhelmed by the number of clients with MPD.

> *As many as one out of one hundred persons could be at risk for multiple personality disorder.*

Dr. Colin Ross, a respected Canadian psychiatrist who specializes in treating multiple personalities, estimates that 5 percent of patients in psychiatric wards in the United States and Canada may have multiple personality disorder. In his book *Multiple Personality Disorder: Diagnosis, Clinical Features, and Treatment,* he theorizes that as many as one out of one hundred persons could be at risk for multiple personality disorder. He came to this figure by determining that 10 percent of the population has experienced severe child abuse, and that 10 percent of all severely abused children could develop multiple personality disorder.[3]

Because females are more likely to be abused as young children, more females than males have multiple personality disorder. Statistically, nine out of ten patients are female.

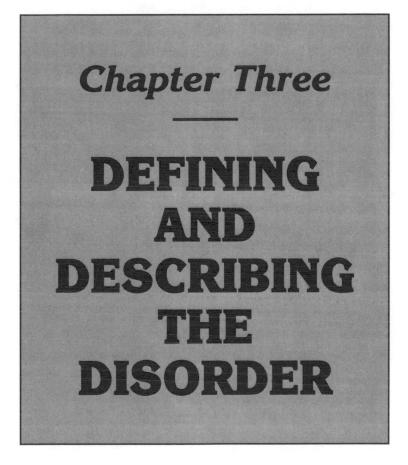

Chapter Three

———

DEFINING AND DESCRIBING THE DISORDER

CONFIRMING A DIAGNOSIS

No name or phrase, such as multiple personality disorder, can adequately describe the variety of emotions, the humanness of the pain, and the drama of the effects of the disorder on families and friends. In the case of MPD, the clinical descriptions leave the depths of personal trauma unknown. If you turn to the latest edition of the *Diagnostic and Statistical Manual of Mental Disorders*[1] (or the *DSM III R* as it is more commonly referred to), you find that this disorder can be summed up in three pages, listing two diagnostic criteria:

1. The existence within the person of two or more distinct personalities or personality states (each with its own relatively enduring patterns of perceiving, relating to, and thinking about the environment and self).

2. At least two of these personalities or personality states recurrently take full control of the person's behavior.

There is much more to this complex disorder. A person with multiple personality disorder (who is called a multiple) has essentially two or more separate personalities within one body.

ORIGINS OF THE DISORDER

Multiple personality disorder is developed in very early childhood—between the ages of two and five. Multiple personality disorder is a *response* to a life-threatening situation. Tragically, it almost always points to extreme child abuse and, in many cases, satanic ritual abuse.

The classic case of multiple personality disorder starts with a child being physically and often sexually abused at the age of two or three or before. The child cannot stop the torture, and there is no rescuer in the wings to save the toddler from the pain. Because the child is so young, she is not able to verbalize what is happening. She certainly is not big enough to fight back physically. The only safe place to go is to take refuge in her mind. The child, who is bright and creative and wants to stay alive, "pretends" herself away and "invents" another personality to take the pain.

This is somewhat similar to the pretend playmates of many children. Pretend playmates are often the extension of a normal (albeit overactive!) imagination—and they are usually the ones blamed for all the mischief in the nursery. In the case of a multiple, the pretend playmate takes the pain instead of just the blame.

A significant aspect of the child abuse experienced is that there is no rescuer. Usually, one parent is the perpetrator of the abuse, but the other is a silent accomplice by virtue of conspicuous noninvolvement and conspiratorial silence. In this environment the child has no es-

> ***In the case of a multiple, the pretend playmate takes the pain instead of just the blame.***

cape, no safe place to hide, which necessitates extreme behavior in order to survive.

When we reconsider the childhood of most people with MPD, this disorder should be easy for us to accept as real rather than meet it with skepticism. The disorder makes sense. A helpless child has few defenses. If we believe that a child is sexually abused and we know the emotional pain it causes, we must believe that something will result from the abuse. It seems only natural that a defenseless child would have to find a way to break away from such a painful reality. The child has only a creative imagination as a tool, and the result is two distinct identities: one was hurt, and the other is free of pain. These two exist side by side until pain hits the pain-free identity. From there, more and more identities must be created for the child to continue to escape the pain. What allows for survival eventually destroys the individual's ability to exist in a real and painful world. But for a time, this splitting away from the pain prevents the child from being overwhelmed by it.

SILENT CONSPIRATORS

These things don't just happen to children; they are *allowed* to happen. Almost always, a parent or relative is aware of the abuse and allows it to continue unabated. Many times it is a parent or relative who perpetrates the abuse.

One of my patients with multiple personality disorder had been molested by her father since she was two years old; on her sixth birthday he began raping her regularly after school until she was in junior high (then the father turned to the younger sisters). I once asked her where her mother was during those events. She told me her mother was usually in the kitchen: "Imagine the horror of being molested the whole time you were in kindergarten through sixth grade and through every incident your mother was cooking dinner and never said anything." I asked her if she thought her mother had some idea of what was going on. She replied rather matter-of-factly, "Well yes, I think she knew what was going on. When I was older and started to make a fuss about it, she would just say, 'Don't aggravate your father. Look at all he's done for you. Give him what he needs.' "

Clearly, the father, the mother, *and* the marriage were sick. The point is that multiple personality disorder doesn't develop in isolation—it is a response not just to pain but to pain in relationship to other family members.

Child abuse is always traumatic, but when there is a known conspiracy to allow it to happen, the pain is much worse. The child is trapped with no one safe to go to for help. It often happens that while one parent or

> *This overwhelming feeling of fear combined with intense emotional pain drives the child into hiding behind new personalities created for the sole purpose of survival.*

stepparent abuses the child, the other parent ignores or pretends to not know what is going on. Often the child will tell the other parent (or another significant caregiver in the home) but is rebuffed or punished for even suggesting what has taken place. The child is not only tortured but abased and made to feel ashamed and responsible for what has happened. The child realizes that adults are not to be trusted or believed and the world is not a safe place for a little child. This overwhelming feeling of fear combined with intense emotional pain drives the child into hiding behind new personalities created for the sole purpose of survival.

ALTERS

The other personalities coinciding in the same body are referred to as *alternate personalities* or *alters*. These alters see themselves as distinctly different not only in personality, but in origin, age, physical description—and even sex! That is, some of the alters see themselves as being male or having long red hair or being a five-year-old child while the actual person is a thirty-six-year-old African-American woman. Each alter may have a distinct accent and refer to completely different memories.

Here are examples of the alters of one of my patients. Carla is a kindergarten teacher in a private school, twenty-nine years old, with long, long "Cinderella" blond hair and a tiny, trim figure. She has a shy, quiet, self-effacing personality.

Carleen is four years old with big blue eyes and curly blond hair. Carleen feels four years old and sees herself as four years old. Everyone around her, though, sees a twenty-nine-year-old carrying a blanket and sucking her thumb. She is terrified of cats but has absolutely no fear of big dogs—in fact, she loves them and will often want to go up to a strange dog to pet it.

C. J. describes himself to be a big burly mountain man with wavy sandy blond hair and a big beard. He likes to ride Harley-Davidsons. He has a foul mouth but is not at all mean or angry, except when he is trying to protect the young children alters. C. J. was "born" when Carla was gang raped in tenth grade while walking home after school through a neighborhood park.

Timmy got his name from a book about a young boy called Busy Timmy. He is now nine years old with big brown eyes and straight brown hair. He is very quiet, very thoughtful, and *very* quick. Timmy is the "escape artist" for any difficult situation. He will lie, steal, cheat, or do anything else necessary to avoid getting a reprimand or blame.

Godiva is named and modeled after the famed Englishwoman. Like Carla, Godiva has long blond hair (naturally, it is longer), and she is much taller than Carla. Godiva is twenty-five, haunts bars and clubs, and loves to sing and dance and be in the spotlight. She is the only one who is left-handed. She is outspoken but also puts the group in jeopardy because of her risky behavior—recreational drug use and one-night stands.

Christine has short-cropped dark brown hair and dark brown eyes. She is twenty-eight years old but comes across as older than her supposed age because of her poise and confidence. She dresses very smartly. She knows a tremendous amount about the world of finance and has worked as a stockbroker. She loves to collect antiques, and she speaks fluent French. Although she works with men, she does not like men sexually because of the things she has seen them do to the others. She says she is a lesbian.

When an alter is "out," the general public sees the outside physique of the multiple. In the case of Carla, people will always see her as the person she is, with long blond hair. When Christine is in charge of the body, she will still *look* like Carla (blond, tiny build, etc.), but she will be dressed in more sophisticated and professional clothes and will exude an air of confident assertiveness.

I asked Christine how it could be that her hair is short and brown when a quick glance in the mirror would indicate her hair is blond. She nonchalantly replied, "Oh

> *Until there has been extensive therapy,* rarely *does the host or actual person know about the alters.*

. . . well, Carla's hair is blond. You see her hair. *My* hair is obviously short and brown.''

Most of the alter personalities know about the host or birth personality. They may refer to her as the outside woman or use her name, and they are aware of her as a person. However, until there has been extensive therapy, *rarely* does the host or actual person know about the alters. She does not know they exist, and when one of them is "out" (meaning in charge of the body and controlling the behavior), she does not know nor remember what happened or what the personality may have done.

IDENTIFYING THE REAL PERSONALITY

As you can imagine, dealing with so many personalities in one body can become very confusing. Sometimes, one of the alters is the predominant or strongest personality and is most often in control of the body. Yet the person whose name is listed on the birth certificate is still referred to as the *core personality*. This *birth* personality of the multiple is the person who first endured the incidents of abuse. This core personality experienced the pain and torture as a very young child—between the ages of two and five or before.

At the first episode of splitting, another personality is invented or imagined into being by the child to handle the pain. This alter will thereafter show up in association with the child's being tortured or abused. This alter is said to be the person who handles pain because that is precisely what he was created to do!

Once this alter makes regular appearances, the original child has a coping mechanism in place for handling other difficult or unsafe situations. The core personality will then create other alters to handle other emotions or special situations. Each alter personality usually deals with one set of specific emotions or area of activity. Only one personality is in charge of the body at any time, and a changing of the guard—when a different personality takes control—is called *switching*. Whichever personality *switches in* to control the body is the personality that will determine the behavior and speech and all other mannerisms of the outside body.

In Carla, I could clearly see how her alters would work to protect her (the core personality) by handling various feelings or situations.

C. J., the mountain man, was there as protector. He also handled anger—he was big and strong enough to defend himself and the child alters and thus could afford the luxury of expressing his anger. The birth or core personality has been unable to express anger without fear of retribution or some kind of reprisal.

Christine was there to handle finances and to make

many of the day-to-day decisions. With Christine in control, factual and clearheaded decisions could be made with regard to money and other vital areas of reality.

Notice the function of Timmy as the escape artist. When a situation came up that might get Carla in trouble (no matter how trivial it may seem to the rest of us— all such situations seem significant to the core personality), Timmy was there to lie, cheat, or steal his way out of Carla's trouble. That his lying or cheating could cause more trouble later was of no concern—his main business was to handle the crisis at hand. Some other alter would have to clean up after him.

DISSOCIATION

The survival and learned response of multiple personality disorder is *dissociation,* and in the psychiatric field, multiple personality disorder is classified as a *dissociative disorder.* The dissociative component, although it saved the multiple in childhood, causes severe problems in later life.

Dissociation itself is not a sign of mental illness or mental disorder. Everyone experiences dissociation to some degree in everyday life. For example, have you ever found yourself daydreaming during a boring class lecture? That is a form of dissociation. It is the ability of the mind to split apart from what is happening in the real world—right in front of you—and to be somewhere else in time and place. Another common example of dissociation is being so lost in thought as you drive along the road that you suddenly realize you have no recollection of the road during the last five minutes and cannot remember all the major milestones (road signs, ramps, and specific scenery).

Dissociation is the ability to "tune out" from the circumstances around you, and multiple personality disor-

> *Dissociation is the ability to "tune out" from the circumstances around you.*

der evokes the ultimate use of dissociation. It is an appropriate and effective way for a young child to tune out pain and to survive the abuse and stay intact in some way. Once it becomes too automatic a response, however, the mind of the multiple will use it for any unpleasant or threatening situation.

Let me illustrate the dynamics of this disorder by means of an analogy. Suppose you have an extremely wealthy woman whose supreme delight in life is her little girl. This woman loves the child tremendously and doesn't wish her to be annoyed or vexed. The mother has in her employ an assortment of nannies and household staff members that she is determined will help her child in every possible way so that she will be a happy, satisfied child.

One day the child cries from frustration because she cannot properly lace and tie her shoes. The mother assigns one of the nannies to tie the little girl's shoes for her so that she won't have to feel frustrated from untied shoes. Later the little girl feels nervous because she cannot finish her math problems. So the mother assigns the household bookkeeper to do the math homework problems. In an attempt to spare the child all of life's pain and humiliation and frustration, the mother thinks she has solved the problem by having her staff deal with the circumstances. Each staff member will handle a problem area according to expertise. Obviously, the child can never grow up because she will never learn to do these things on her own.

In a like manner, the person with MPD can never mature because her mind will split into another personality to handle a problem before the core personality can learn to solve it on *her* own. She never learns to get over any psychological hurdle on her own when she depends on dissociation.

MENTAL ILLNESS OR MENTAL DISORDER?

There is some debate over using the term *mental illness* when describing multiple personality disorder. In a certain sense, to have multiple personality disorder would not be considered to be mentally *healthy* since it is a dysfunctional way of living. With this perspective in mind, it is appropriately referred to as a mental *illness.*

On the other hand, some feel that multiple personality disorder is unique and adaptive and therefore should not be referred to as a mental illness but rather as a unique giftedness.

Although there may be a biological component to

one's capacity to dissociate involved, multiple personality disorder is primarily a special *learned response* that becomes a lifelong coping mechanism to any threatening situation. In this sense, multiple personality disorder is seen as a disorder rather than an illness, and in the *DSM III R,* multiple personality disorder is classified as a *disorder.* This distinction has held great importance for some of my patients. The fear of being mentally ill has kept many people from seeking help and getting psychiatric treatment. Rather than feel sorry for or look down at my patients, I marvel at their survival and the intricacy of their minds' capabilities. They are definitely gifted to have come through so much in their past.

LOSS OF CONTROL

People with multiple personality disorder are not insane, but they are often afraid they are because their world makes no sense. Things that are happening to them do not happen to other people. Consider these typical experiences of my patients:

- Carla finds expensive, classy clothes in her closet. She knows she didn't buy them, but they are all in her size. The dresses are in bold, striking colors, quite unlike the gentle pastel flowered frocks she would pick out for herself.

- Regina constantly hears voices in her head. Some of them have names. They are frequently arguing, and she can hear these voices making critical comments about her.

- Naomi Jo often finds herself in the driver's seat and doesn't remember how she got there or where she is going. She tells me that the last thing she remembers is being in class at the local state university. The next moment she "awakens" to find she is in her car on the freeway—and it's three hours later! She has no idea what she is doing there or where she was going.

What all of these patients have in common is that *they do not feel in control of their lives.* Something is out of place, and strange things are going on. They don't want to be crazy. My patients are not isolated examples in this regard. Multiples are usually very intelligent people with an ability to reason. They realize that these experiences, however commonplace and familiar for them, would be considered out of the ordinary for other people. They innately know that it is *not* normal, and they are very fearful that they are going crazy.

> *Multiples are usually very in-telligent people with an ability to reason.*

When people with multiple personality disorder come into therapy, they are reluctant to be completely candid, partially because what they are describing has lots of gaps and holes and makes no sense. Because of their early abuse, it is also difficult for them to trust authority figures. They may not even remember the abuse, but the pattern of distrust of authority is well established. In this regard let me contrast here patients with MPD and patients who have a more traditional mental illness. A person with schizophrenia, for instance, can describe illogical, irrational experiences, but they believe and express these actions as if they were completely normal. Host personalities are aware that something is amiss in their world. A multiple will seriously consider whether her behavior could be irrational. This is a good sign (even though her behavior may be incredibly bizarre).

Often at this point, the person with MPD decides to enter meaningful therapy. She gambles that at least *knowing* what is wrong will be better than living in uncertainty.

SUMMARY

Multiple personality disorder is probably one of the most baffling, yet most interesting mental health problem. It is a coping mechanism that in turn becomes a learned response that in turn becomes a roadblock to emotional maturity. Multiple personality disorder is an ongoing, chronic disorder, which will stay with the person for life. It is not something that the person will outgrow—if anything, it will get worse. It can be a terrifying and bewildering experience for the multiple when she doesn't know what is happening with her life and she feels out of control. Although multiple personality disorder was initially a response to protect the person from pain in early life, the disorder causes confusion, anguish, and a different kind of pain in later life.

In spite of how disruptive and dysfunctional the disorder seems, it is a treatable disorder. The prognosis for a successful recovery is good, provided the patient has a competent doctor or therapist and no major obstacles outside the disorder. People who have a family member or friend with multiple personality disorder can be encouraged that there is definitely hope for a more ordinary existence.

Chapter Four

_____

MARIEELENA'S STORY

THE REFERRAL

MarieElena was referred to me by her parish priest with whom she had been in counseling for more than two and a half years. She was very intelligent—I would have described her as gifted—and she had razor cuts all over her arms, thighs, and abdomen.

MarieElena had been feeling suicidal. She could not identify where the self-destructive feelings originated or why they occurred at that point in her life. No single personal crisis would have left her wanting to die.

Her parish priest thought she might be going through a stage of adjustment to the Los Angeles area since she had moved to LA from a small city in northern California. MarieElena couldn't afford to go to professional counseling, and since she wasn't clear on exactly what was troubling her, Father William thought some congenial pastoral counseling would put her at ease. However, MarieElena became increasingly nonfunctional and withdrawn. She started to complain about strange flashbacks and migrainelike headaches. She was taking what I considered a dangerous level of over-the-counter pain killers for her headaches, but nothing seemed to dent

> *The threat of fire made me a bit anxious. Perhaps the weather was a harbinger of what I would uncover with MarieElena.*

them. Father William decided that since her condition was getting worse, he was not competent to help her, and he began looking for someone better equipped to handle her case.

I took the referral, and she came into my office on a Thursday afternoon in October—a warm Santa Ana-wind day that in California is likely to be the precursor to a brush fire. These kinds of days always give me the feeling of anticipation, that something exciting or unusual is about to happen. I guess the threat of fire made me a bit anxious. Perhaps the weather was a harbinger of what I would uncover with MarieElena.

THE ASSESSMENT

The first thing I found remarkable when trying to take down a comprehensive history for my new patient was that there wasn't any history—at least of childhood. She couldn't remember anything in her life before the age of fourteen. She remembered that she had a dog named Ralph, a big Irish setter, and that her parents had a gray house at the end of a long cul-de-sac. MarieElena also remembered going to a birthday party at the house of a friend of her brothers. Other than that, she knew absolutely nothing about her early past.

The other curious thing I noted was that she was devoid of appropriate emotional responses. One of her complaints was that she "didn't feel anything." She had a very detached manner of discussing herself, as though she were an outside observer commenting on a friend.

MarieElena was a shoe buyer for a large department store chain in the San Fernando Valley, and she had previously managed the women's fine clothing department in a store north of San Francisco. She had never been married but had several relationships, including one engagement that she broke off six years ago. All of that she also discussed in a flat, monotone voice.

I was intrigued but perplexed. Nothing seemed exactly *wrong* with MarieElena, but something definitely wasn't right.

UNCOVERING MPD

At a later session, she talked about recurring flashbacks of events she claimed she knew nothing about. The flashbacks consisted of things and images that didn't make sense to her. In one scenario, she was covered, nearly smothered, in white sheets. She couldn't breathe, and when she tried to reach out to push away the sheets, she couldn't stretch her arms; they were all wrapped up in sheets as well. In another scenario, she was hiding in a dark, cramped area, perhaps under a house or in a basement, and she knew she was terrified for her life.

MarieElena was overwhelmed with certain tactile responses that she couldn't explain, either. She would distinctly feel the texture of cloth over her face and would touch her hand to her cheek to find nothing there. The specific sensation was always accompanied by feelings of fear and anxiety.

As she was telling me all that, she pushed up the right sleeve of her shirt to look at her watch. She was left-handed. The red scars didn't escape me.

"Tell me about your scars," I said. "When did you do that?"

She looked at me with an almost dumbfounded expression, as though it was the first she had seen or heard about the self-inflicted wounds. She extended her left arm and demonstrated the same cut marks on her fore-arm and side of the wrist. I suspected they were self-inflicted. Slowly MarieElena pulled up her shirt sleeve to reveal numerous inch-long red scars or scratches across her arms. In a very soft voice she said, "Sometimes we cut ourselves to know it's real."

I could hear in my memory the voice of one of my professors years ago in medical school: "Whenever you have dissociators, look for cutting or burning. Self-mutilation happens as a refocusing mechanism for those that are cut off from their feelings or memories." I was sure that was happening here.

MarieElena's use of "we" didn't escape me. Lorinda immediately came to mind. I tried to establish a connection between her amnesia, her tactile terrors, the episode of smothering, and the cutting. I was fairly certain I wasn't dealing with a condition such as schizophrenia,

> *In a very soft voice she said, "Sometimes we cut ourselves to know it's real."*

but I needed to find the root of the problem. I could tell she was a deeply troubled young woman, and I hoped I could help her.

MarieElena was a mystery I wanted to solve. I asked her to keep a journal to record what she did during the day as well as her thoughts and feelings that might accompany her various activities and events.

MARIEELENA'S FAMILY

The following sessions were relatively uneventful. I took down more current history: her employment, her paintings (she did spectacular oils at home in her free time), and any augmentation she could give me about her family.

Two older brothers lived in northern California. MarieElena's father had died of a heart attack when she was twenty-two. Her mother had been diagnosed as having schizophrenia two years later and was in a mental hospital in Camarillo, about sixty miles north of Los Angeles. MarieElena would visit her once a month; she described her mother's illness as a detached clinical observer would have done. No, it didn't bother her that her mother was mentally ill; those things couldn't be helped. There was no one to take care of the mother full-time, but she wasn't a burden—MarieElena's father's estate covered the bills.

Her mother's illness was bound to be tied in with some of MarieElena's problems, I thought. I determined to look further into the subject.

What MarieElena could remember was that they were an ordinary family. Her mother was active in the high-school PTA. She was rather supportive of all the children and constantly encouraged them to succeed. Father was a quiet man; he worked at a regional winery in the bot-tling and shipping department. They went to Sunday Mass each week; the mother was an especially devout churchgoer.

THE JOURNAL

Several weeks after I had started working with MarieElena, I asked to review her journal at the end of our session. I planned to take it home with me to read over the weekend.

The next day, I stretched out on my living room couch and opened her notebook. I skimmed the first three pages, which were uneventful but immediately supportive of my suspicions of multiple personality dis-order. MarieElena had a small, tidy handscript that leaned to the right. On the third page, there was a dis-tinctly different handwriting. The entry stated, "She's always worried about what the mother might think. She ought to just let Anne out so we can all have some fun. We hate that she's always depressed."

I figured there was very little chance that MarieElena

> *MarieElena had a small, tidy handscript that leaned to the right. On the third page, there was a distinctly different handwriting.*

had lent the book to a close friend or coworker to ask for feedback or observations. Suspecting MPD, I felt that most likely, Anne was another personality.

Two pages later, the rounded handwriting appeared again: "We would all like to go back to northern California. The children are not safe in southern California. When will she learn she doesn't owe her mother anything. Let the brothers try spending one day with the mother."

A third handwriting—a sloppy scrawl—followed next: "Harmony should speak for herself. Southern California is fine with me. But, why doesn't the woman get out and LIVE?"

One entry was printed in a young child's block lettering: "I would like some crayons. She never has crayons. MarieElena's pens aren't good. I need different colors. I wish I had a doll."

Another entry read, "Somebody has simply GOT to do something about Chester. I am sick of his OVERREACT-

ING at every little incident. His fighting is surely going to get us all in trouble.''

I read rapidly back and forth to notice the differences in the entries. Then I read through the next several pages as they revealed different personalities with original handwritings. I had little experience but a lot of motivation to help.

Chapter Five

———

FEATURES AND CHARAC-TERISTICS

PATIENT PROFILE

MarieElena is typical of most multiple personality disorder patients. The disorder may be first exhibited in early childhood, but it may not be detected clinically until individuals are around thirty years of age. As previously discussed, most all of the patients seen in therapy are female.

People with undiagnosed multiple personality disorder come into therapy for complaints about depression, suicide, drug or alcohol abuse, generalized anxiety, or even insomnia. Some start to sense the nature of the problem due to movies seen or books read. None of my patients have entered therapy knowing what they have. Only 5 percent of persons with MPD are knowledgeable enough to make a self-diagnosis beforehand. I have seen several people who thought that they might have the disorder, but they didn't. One was using the idea of the disorder as an excuse for her behavior. These pseudo-multiples often are part of the reason the validity of the disorder is questioned.

That MarieElena was only now realizing she couldn't recall her years before fourteen is evidence of some tim-

> *Only 5 percent of persons with MPD are knowledgeable enough to make a self-diagnosis beforehand.*

ing mechanism the mind uses to block out the past, perhaps to protect itself before it can allow itself to face what happened and process it. It is a remarkable tool of self-preservation. I've observed that people who have undergone abuse during childhood are amnesiac for those years of abuse. That is especially true for girls who have been sexually abused. Later, when the mind is more able to handle some repair work, the memories return, and often detailed flashbacks or other emotional problems related to the abuse start to slowly surface. For some multiples, these memories crop up in the twenties or earlier. But multiples usually start appearing in therapy between the ages of thirty and forty. Of course, some are much younger and some are quite older, but the average age for diagnosis is between twenty-eight and thirty-eight.

HEADACHE

MarieElena's headache is another very, very common complaint heard from patients with MPD. My patients describe these headaches as being "like migraines," but unlike migraines, they do not respond to conventional medication. The headaches are frequent and recurrent and can also often precede switching between the alter personalities.

MISSING TIME AND MEMORIES

For persons with multiple personality disorder, the missing childhood is a fairly standard feature. The abuse is too painful for them to handle, so the host has no memory of it. The memory lies with each of the alters.

> *The headaches are frequent and recurrent and can also often precede switching between the alter personalities.*

When patients with MPD describe lost time or blank spells during their *day-to-day* activities, they refer to a time in which another alter is out or in control and the host or core personality has no awareness of it. A patient may comment,

- "I seem to have a problem with time. It doesn't move normally for me."

- "Hardly a week goes by that I don't have several blank spots in which I can't remember what I have done."

- "People are always accusing me of doing or saying things that I know I wouldn't ever do!"

I usually consider missing time to be a tip-off to at least *suspect* multiple personality disorder and to look for other diagnostic criteria. My patients have had blank spells lasting for days, weeks, or even months.

Obviously, this amnesia or missing time element can be extremely disruptive in the multiple's ability to function in everyday life. Not all multiples miss time every single day; it depends on the severity of the disorder. Some multiples may go through several personalities in one day. Others may go for several days or weeks before switching into another personality.

For the core personality, the confusion comes when she wakes up after a blank spell (which was when an alter was out) and has no recollection of what she did or said during the previous time period. MarieElena told me that over the years her friends would say she had said or done things that she not only could not remember but adamantly *knew* she hadn't said or done. They were behaviors that were out of character for her. As she was to discover later, her alters did the actions during her blackout periods.

Blackout periods also explain why persons with MPD are so often accused of being liars. They disavow any knowledge of having done or said something to which everyone else was a witness. The fact was, they *didn't* do or say it—an alter was in control of the body at the time, and naturally, the multiple had no recollection of what the other personality did or said.

The confusion from these blackouts often motivates people to seek help and at times tips them off to the nature of their problem. One multiple had studied psychology and obtained her master's degree in marriage and family counseling. Part of her motivation for a profession in psychology and counseling was to gain greater insight into her problems of feeling detached and remote from others and from herself. After completing her studies, she was more in touch with her feelings, but she was convinced there was something very different about herself that she couldn't figure out. Her greatest clue came one night when she was with her brother and sister-in-law. She sat down to eat and in front of her was a huge porterhouse steak so rare that the red juices made her nauseated. Just as she was about to gag, her sister-in-law told her she had attempted to prepare her favorite cut of beef rare just like she requested over the phone the night before.

The patient had no recollection of a conversation with her sister-in-law the night before. Furthermore, she had stopped eating all red meat and ate only fish and chicken. As most multiples do, she attempted to hide her confusion. Her biggest dilemma was that she could not eat the blood-rare piece of meat. She quickly decided to feign illness, leave the table and retreat into the bathroom. The raw meat before her made it easy for her. She did feel sick. She finished the evening without eating.

The incident convinced her of one of three things. She thought she might be losing her memory; perhaps even Alzheimer's was setting in young. If it wasn't that, she might be losing her mind. Her third alternative was that she might have MPD. The three options were all terrifying to her. She sought the counsel of a psychiatrist to assist in unraveling the confusion and the missing pieces brought on by the blackout periods.

VOICES

Although hearing voices is a predominant characteristic of MPD, not everyone experiences it, at least not at first. This one feature of the disorder causes more multiples to feel like they are going crazy than anything else. It, too, is a great motivator for multiples to seek treatment.

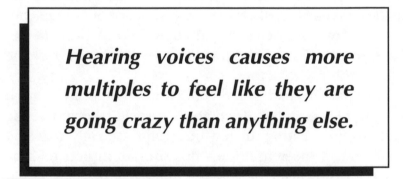

Hearing voices causes more multiples to feel like they are going crazy than anything else.

MarieElena did not complain initially about hearing voices. Patients are often reluctant to bring up this subject out of fear of being rejected or labeled. Only after trust and rapport have been established does the patient feel confident enough to reveal this secret. As a psychiatrist who has dealt with all kinds of mental illnesses and disorders, I point out to my multiple patients that *their* voices *are* different.

When my schizophrenic or psychotic patients talk

about voices, they are hearing them *outside* their heads (i.e., around the corner, from the next room, or from an inanimate object). These voices are disjunct, they make no sense, and they are sometimes incoherent. They may order the patient to do something in relation to the patient's reality that is destructive, and the person with schizophrenia often feels duty bound to obey this commanding voice. For multiples, the voices come from *inside* their heads. The voices are lucid and intelligent, and they hold rational conversations. Each voice has a specific personality—it is believed that these voices are the various alter personalities that exist within the multiple. They do not control the multiple, although she may choose to react to something she hears them saying.

Regina could hear two female voices/personalities always criticizing the clothing she was wearing or the decisions she was making. She could distinguish several other voices, including one male, holding lively conversations among themselves. Sometimes, the voices were so noisy with their bickering and arguing and trying to talk all at once that Regina described it as a "loud roar" in her head. The roar and confusion of nonstop voices can be extraordinarily distracting and interfere with concentration and thinking.

INTELLIGENCE AND CREATIVITY

I have noted that every one of my patients with multiple personality disorder is an extremely bright and creative individual. Research studies on multiples bear this out and show that multiples frequently test in the gifted or genius range on intelligence tests.[1] Sybil, the woman with MPD whose story was written up in the famous book by the same name, was reported as having an IQ of 170.

Multiples who have not gone to college are extraordinarily knowledgeable about a myriad of subjects. On the whole, they read *a lot.* Each alter is reading, and each alter is pursuing subjects of interest. The resulting composite of all these intelligent personalities is a person who knows a tremendous amount of information on a variety of subjects. You might say that a multiple knows enough information for several people, which is exactly right!

People with MPD are also very gifted in the creative sense—as writers, painters, and artists. One of my recent patients who is suspected of having MPD wrote several excellent poems in her journal. When I commented on her impressive ability, she said that it was the first time she had ever written a poem. Here is an example of how well she can communicate through poetry:

> To and fro,
> to and fro,
> where she stops
> nobody knows—
> with the spin of the head
> and a countdown is said,
> who will she be this time?
>
> To and fro,
> to and fro,
> where she stops
> I'd like to know.
> The feelings change

at the drop of a hat.
One moment I feel this,
the next I feel that.
How do I pin down
the feelings inside
and bring them together
so they will no longer hide?

When one sees the other,
they'll start to fight;
the ones that are mean
fight with all their might,
but the ones that are scared
will run and hide out of sight.

Confusion, confusion,
is all that I hear,
voice upon voice
ring in my ear.
I cover my ear
but to no avail.

. . . .

To die, to die,
is all I think of.
But would I go to hell
or heaven above?
Would I do it? Could I do it?
Should I do it? Why?
To find peace and relief
in the sweet by-and-by.

The innate intelligence and giftedness of persons with MPD allowed them to find a creative solution to the original abuse situation. Their enormous creativity invented the only possible escape route from the pain and abuse—into the mind. While many of us would have fantasized a knight in shining armor that we wished could come along and help us, persons with MPD have created means to rescue themselves from the horror by having "someone else" experience it instead of them.

KEEN MEMORY

Despite lapses of time and periods of amnesia, people with MPD have extraordinary and remarkable memories because each alter has a separate and distinct memory. A multiple's mind and body have been so traumatized that they are acutely sensitive to the least of stimuli. Therefore, a multiple recalling an incident can remember with all five senses. One of my patients was recalling her abuse, and while she was describing her burns, red welts rose on her arm at the original site of her burns!

> *One of my patients was recalling her abuse, and while she was describing her burns, red welts rose on her arm at the original site of her burns!*

Features and Characteristics

While I have not seen this myself, I have heard reports from reliable colleagues regarding phenomenon such as bleeding from the hands or the nose in association with recollection of abuse. Since the abuse may occur in a preverbal period of time (before the child has mastered talking), the memories may not be held as thoughts or ideas that have words to go with them. The body remembers, however, and the memories are keen and sharp but may be visual scenes (flashbacks), sounds, smells or feelings, physical sensations, and emotional states.

SENSITIVITY

This extreme physical sensitivity transcends to other areas as well. Multiples have a built-in antenna that picks up subtle emotions and feelings and gestures of others. They have an uncanny ability to "read" people—almost as though they know what you are thinking before you express it. They are quick to feel any hesitancy due to disbelief on the part of the therapist, and they are especially adept at sensing whether or not someone is being up front with them. One famous psychiatrist, Dr. David Caul, described multiples as having the ability to "smell a liar a million miles away."[2]

For this reason, I let them know a bit of what is happening in my world. I know they will sense if I am feeling the least bit distracted—and they often misunderstand and take it personally. So I often confess when I am distracted or when something unrelated to them is weighing on my mind. Then I say, "I want to let you know what is going on with me. Now we have this time scheduled together, and I want to put that aside so I can concentrate on you and how you are doing."

In this manner they know that if my attention is not completely theirs for a split second, the reasons have nothing to do with them. It also allows them to know that I am truly interested in them and want to be focused on them during our time together.

EASILY HYPNOTIZED

Multiples have been noted to be highly hypnotizable. Dissociation is an altered state of consciousness, and therefore is, in a certain sense, a form of self-hypnosis. And since multiples have developed dissociation into an art form, it would follow that they could be hypnotized easily. For those with MPD, hypnosis can be used to quickly access information and memories during therapy more rapidly than through conventional psychotherapy.

MIND OVER MATTER

One of the most fascinating aspects of MPD is the "mind over matter" phenomenon, or the plasticity of the body in relation to the mind. The body of a multiple will literally undergo physiological changes depending on which alter is in control of the body!

Although the next chapter will deal more thoroughly with alters, I include this information here because this aspect can be a telltale sign of the secondary personality—the definitive verification of the disorder.

In the case of MarieElena, that is exactly what hap-

> *The body of a multiple will literally undergo physiological changes depending on which alter is in control of the body!*

pened. After I had read the journal and noted the very different handwritings and personalities, I was about 90 percent certain she had MPD. I observed carefully to see if she displayed any other signs or symptoms that would confirm the diagnosis.

UNIQUE CHARACTERISTICS OF THE ALTERS

One day MarieElena came into her session very upbeat—almost bubbly. I asked her why she was so happy and full of life. Since not all of a multiple's personalities are extremes of each other like Dr. Jekyll and Mr. Hyde, this could have just been MarieElena in a very good mood, but I suspected it was more. She told me about a lot of very pleasant things that were going on with her school and about a new oil painting class she was taking through adult education. All of that made sense, and I was mostly pleased that she seemed to have pulled out of her doldrums. At the end of the session, she needed to sign some papers. As she searched through her purse for a pen, I went behind my desk, pulled one out of the drawer, and tossed it over to her. She reached out her right hand and snapped it up expertly between her thumb and forefinger. Next she leaned forward to sign the papers on my desk. Something was buzzing off in the back of my mind that I couldn't get a hold of. Then I realized what it was. The MarieElena I had been treating was *left*-handed.

Multiples usually have at least one personality with opposite handedness, and each alter has distinct handwriting, as unique as the individual personality. Each alter has a heart rate, visual acuity and field, EEG, PET scan, voice print, and even allergy sensitivities unique to that personality. One alter may require glasses, while none of the others, including the core personality, have any vision problems.

Some alters have illnesses or require special medications that none of the other personalities need. In other cases, an alter may be allergic to a particular medication. If that alter comes out after the core personality or another alter has taken such a medication, the results can be disastrous. A real problem exists when a child alter comes out after one of the adult alters has taken an adult strength medication or has been drinking. The youngster will be under the influence of too large a dose and may get sick![3]

These physiological changes that are verifiable by scientific methods help to validate MPD for all of those who are involved with the diagnosis and treatment. They help the multiple to understand her disorder and how it affects her physically. Such data are useful to the family or friends of the multiple who are afraid that multiple personality disorder doesn't *really* exist. The data can also verify the complexity of the problem and the unlikelihood that the person will be able to quickly snap out of it.

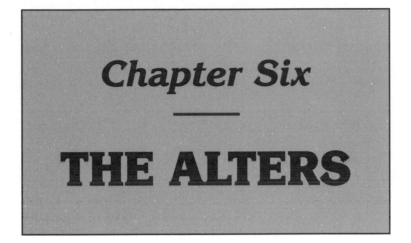

Chapter Six

THE ALTERS

VERONICA

When I received a call that Regina couldn't make her appointment for the afternoon, I felt a sense of relief. I had to go over my notes to prepare for a court appearance two days away, and I would have a little more time. I worked through lunch.

At two-twenty-five, my secretary knocked on the door. "Dr. Clark, your two-thirty is here?" she stated quizzically. I looked down at my schedule.

"That's Regina—but she canceled?" I countered with the same question at the end of my statement.

"That's what I thought, doctor, but she *is* here. What do you want me to say to her?"

"Okay, I'll see her." I started to make neat piles of the files I was reviewing while I waited for Regina. She was a hyper, somewhat self-centered aggressive woman-on-the-go. I had been seeing her about two months. She had come in for unspecific anxieties and slight depression, probably due to stress. I admired Regina for her creativity and her drive, but I was concerned about her overdoing it all. Although she talked a great deal, she hadn't opened up at all personally, so I wondered if she didn't just need more time to build an alliance with me. I hoped she could reveal the truth about herself once she fully trusted me. Regina had a real flair for the dramatic and was always dressed in bright, trendy clothes. I simultaneously braced myself for, and looked forward to, her grand entrance.

"Dr. Clark, good afternoon! I am very pleased to finally be able to meet you in person."

Since I didn't recognize the voice, I looked up and did a double take. Regina looked about forty-five years old (she is a young-looking thirty-three). She had her blond hair styled straight and parted on the side and swept down over one eye a la Veronica Lake. It's usually set with large lively curls a la Farrah Fawcett circa 1977. She had on a very sophisticated, very expensive black-and-gray dress (she usually wore the latest yuppie skirt and shirt fashions).

There was a slight chance that Regina was attempting to be dramatic, take me off guard, or be funny. There was also a slight possibility that she was showing off her expensive new clothes. But with my growing awareness of multiple personality disorder, I immediately thought of the possibility that I was with an alter of Regina, even though she had not yet been diagnosed as having MPD.

Playing along, I replied in gracious fashion while extending my hand, "And to whom do I owe this honor?"

"Veronica," she oozed. (*Yes,* I thought, *it* was *Veronica Lake. Okay, good imitation.*)

"Oh, yes, Veronica Lake. Please sit down." I gestured toward the couch.

She moved elegantly backward onto the couch and smoothed her hair self-assuredly off her face. "Oh, please," she laughed knowingly. "Not the Veronica Lake jokes from *you,* too. It's Veronica Daniels. Here.'' She plucked out a small pinkish card from her tiny black purse and handed it to me.

The pale pink card with gray printing and sophisticated type style read:

Veronica Daniels
Fine Art Consultant
Specializing in European Botanical Prints

The card further confirmed my suspicion of MPD. If I had just met the woman before me, I would have characterized her as a high-society middle-aged woman, probably married to a wealthy man, dabbling in the arts trade as an intellectual part-time hobby. In fact, Regina was single and worked fifty to sixty hours a week as assistant producer for one of the many small successful production studios throughout the Los Angeles area.

Veronica continued in a smooth, calm, carefree manner: "Regina is taking a few days off from work—mental health vacation days. That is why I called to cancel *her* appointment, and I figured we might get a chance to talk instead. I'm concerned about her overinvolvement, overworking, overstressed *everything.* She's working herself to death.''

Although I had treated patients with multiple personality, I hadn't experienced an alter change that was so profound in a while. As she continued with her conversation, I studied Veronica with fascination. I kept trying to see if Regina was playacting a role, but it was truly more than a matter of someone trying to use a different voice. Veronica's subtle gestures and vocal inflections were uniquely different from Regina's. Veronica looked like, yet was different from, Regina in the same way that an older sister can remarkably resemble a sibling, yet remains a separate individual. Veronica was a very classy alter personality of Regina.

On more than one occasion I have found myself so caught off guard as I was this time. Each time I am amazed and fascinated. It is the same body of the patient I have known and been treating, but there is someone else, someone new in the room with me and not the same person I have known thus far. It gives me an eerie feeling and has at times made the hair on the back of my neck stand up.

ALTERNATE PERSONALITIES

The alternate personalities are the manifestation of the multiple's fragmentation and dissociation in MPD. They are most interesting and the most mysterious aspect of the disorder.

One of the repeated descriptions about alters by the mental health community is that they are not "separate people."[1] However, they are separate *personalities,* embodied in a single person. The same brain that belongs to the core personality is the mastermind behind the alter personalities. These alters have unique tastes, interests, and styles, and a unique set of separate memories. As indicated previously, they have separate IQs, vision, heart rates, and other individualized physical mannerisms and responses. It is not known yet how this happens.

Biographies of people with MPD report that the alters can speak, read, and write foreign languages unknown to the core personality. They are accomplished in spe-

> *The same brain that belongs to the core personality is the mastermind behind the alter personalities.*

cific knowledge and skills not shared (ostensibly) by the multiple. I need to make it clear that this is not spontaneous knowledge. If we remember that the multiple is an exceptionally intelligent and highly creative individual, these skills are the raw material or capabilities available for the alter to draw upon. The alter, as a separate personality, engages in behavior not known or remembered by the multiple. Therefore, the alter (with a voracious appetite for information and knowledge) can become well versed in a subject that is unique to his or her personality, independent of the multiple.

Veronica was obviously a refined, well-educated, and sophisticated alter personality. She had a real love of art, especially old European prints. She was self-studied on the subject but was thoroughly knowledgeable. Apparently, Veronica had a consulting business whenever she was in control of the body. I wondered how she could possibly transact business with Regina's busy schedule.

I found out as Veronica shared this story: Veronica did most of her work part-time on the weekends. She made connections with clients through galleries with which she had set up special business arrangements. She worked with about five main galleries—one in Santa Barbara, one in Ojai, and a few in the Pasadena area. She also had an arrangement with one gallery to use its phone number on her business cards.

I began to see that some of Regina's complaints about always messing her time up and not getting things done on the weekends were not a matter of overwork. Regina was not around to get things done.

PURPOSES

As inventions of the creative mind of the multiple, alters are essentially *tools* used by the multiple for protection. Psychologist Jim Friesen proposes that within their capacity to protect the host personality, there are four different purposes for which alters are created.[2]

1. To Dissociate from Trauma

The multiple assigns an entire event—the pain and the memory—to an alternate personality. The alter protects the multiple by taking the pain and any remembrance of the event. Dissociation is different from suppression, in which one tries to avoid thinking about or to forget about a situation. In dissociation, the memory does not exist for the host; it belongs completely to the alter. The event did not happen to the core personality —it happened to the alter.

2. To Model an Important Person

In this function, an alter is created that is modeled after another person or a fictional character who has some significant trait that the alter will incorporate. Most often the alter personality will model a parent or an authority figure. This may be a stern personality that comes out to berate or scold or punish other people in the life of the multiple. Other examples are fictional characters who represent certain qualities or ideals that are being emulated. For instance, one patient's alter was called Superman. The alter had great strength and came into the multiple's life to rescue her and defend her from an unpleasant and abusive situation.

3. To Cope with New Life Situations

These alters come into being when the person with MPD is faced with a new situation that is perceived as threatening. It does not have to be a dangerous or physically abusive situation. The fact that it is unfamiliar territory, which the multiple doesn't know how to handle, is sufficient reason to be threatening. Examples of these situations include getting married, when a new alternate personality is created to take on the role of spouse, enrolling in a new class, finding a new job, or doing anything in a new environment.

4. To Carry Out the Desires of a Cult

Underground satanic cults use torture and brainwashing methods to *intentionally* create alters in young children. These alters learn to respond to the suggestions or stimuli of the cult in order to carry out specific functions later on as older children and as adults.

> *Underground satanic cults use torture and brainwashing methods to* intentionally *create alters in young children.*

TYPES OF ALTERS

Within these four roles or purposes, numerous types of alters occur in MPD.

Child

Almost all multiples have child alters—personalities under the age of twelve. They behave completely as any child would. They suck their thumbs, twist their hair, like to eat cookies, throw tantrums, and use childlike vocabulary. When these child alters surface, they seem to shrink the adult body they are in and really do appear to get younger and smaller! However, unlike real children, they have an uncanny understanding of adult concepts when I am in a discussion with them about the multiple or another alter personality. I have found that like other children, they give refreshingly frank and honest answers. That often helps me obtain useful information about the system of alters and how they function.[3]

Persecutor

The persecutor alter is a violent, angry alter who is always self-destructive. The persecutor will take drugs, engage in dangerous behavior, attempt suicide, and in general put the multiple at risk through various unsafe situations.

For instance, the persecutor alter for a male multiple will start a fight in a bar because of his belligerent personality. He will pick a fight with a gang member with the likelihood that he will have to try to take on the whole gang. He is also likely to abuse alcohol or any other drug.

In a female, the persecutor might regularly go to a nightclub in an unsafe neighborhood, engage in prostitution or act promiscuously, or take drugs. Godiva, who was an alter of my patient Carla, was a persecutor. She would constantly put Carla (and the other alters) at risk by picking up men for one-night stands. Godiva used drugs indiscriminately—she would take drugs as though they were nothing more than candy. She had a frivolous, terribly irresponsible character and frequently would mouth off at authority figures.

Rescuer

The rescuer is like First Officer Spock from *Star Trek*. Usually devoid of emotion, this alter is also the logical one. This alter is able, proficient, and responsible—and will keep the corporate structure together, so to speak.

Christine would be considered the rescuer alter personality for Carla. Christine had a very good head for numbers and most often handled the financial aspects for Carla—balancing the checkbook, saving money, and so on. She searched the want ads for appropriate positions for Carla.

Helper

This alter could be considered a type of rescuer, but the helper plays a much more predominant position within the multiple's life. Much speculation and controversy center on the helper, who is also referred to as the inner self helper, or ISH.[4] The ISH is sometimes considered to be an entity and not an actual alter. Not every therapist has uncovered this alter because the ISH does not come out like other presenting personalities—the ISH is an observer, not a doer. This helper comes out during therapy.

Uncovering an ISH can be a tremendous benefit to the therapist because the ISH has a complete history and knowledge of the multiple. For this reason, therapists also refer to the ISH as a memory trace. The ISH has information about when the other alters were created and what incidents or situations brought them forth.

Those who are inexperienced working with people with MPD have interesting explanations for this inner self helper. The most frequent explanation is that it is an angel who has come to fight the destructive forces of evil. Before you completely dismiss the spiritual implications here, consider that there are such a depth of spiri-

> ***The most frequent explanation is that the ISH is an angel who has come to fight the destructive forces of evil.***

tual discernment and such a need to be nurtured after these cruelties of abuse that a loving God could send a loving spirit to assist in preserving and healing the multiple.

ALTERS ON THEIR OWN

Limited emotional response also points to the *incompleteness* of alters and the fact that they are just personalities. They are a fragmentation of the core personality but certainly not complete individuals in and of themselves. They were created to help the central figure.

The alters never take over and absorb the core personality. I find that they are more often (except for the persecutor) supportive of the multiple. I envision the alters like psychological guards standing about the multiple. Each one has a different area to protect and function to perform in defense of the multiple.

Alters do not age in the traditional sense. That is, they do not get one year older each year. A year and a half may pass, and an alter will tell me that she is still the same age. Some of the children alters do not age at all. Although alters are more often younger than the multiple, I have also come across alters who are older than the original personality.

It is important to note that alters have problems, too. They are not perfect or all-good or all-knowledgeable. They have strengths and weaknesses. They can be sneaky, and they can be devious, but they almost always operate from *fear.* Fear of pain. Fear of being found out.

Alters could also be considered the *present* expression of some *past* event for the multiple. The alters keep the memory and act out the related emotion. At first, the alters seem so different from one another, but when we examine more closely their purposes and functions within the multiple's system, we see that alters are interrelated.

For instance, alters often have a paired relationship— a responsible and irresponsible or an impulsive and cautious pair. If the impulsive personality responds to a threatening situation, the alter will act out externally by fighting back or running away. If the more cautious reasoning personality comes forward, she will handle the situation by thinking about it and making a plan, or she will bravely stick her chin out and quietly accept rebuke or pain.

Within the organization of the mind, the alters are related on a broader sense through trauma (the original events) and emotions. After a time in treatment with one who is progressing well, my patient (or one of the alters actually) will draw me a map of the alters and how they are perceived to be related, along with other pertinent information (such as their "birth dates" and the episode or event that caused their coming into being).

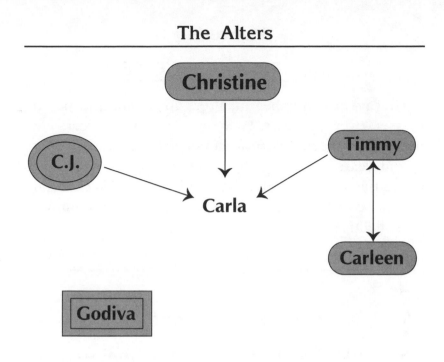

Map drawn by Christine showing the relationships of the alters to Carla.

In this alter map, we can see that Carla, the host personality, is protected by three alters: Christine (the logical, responsible one who makes all the major decisions), C. J. (who has the brute strength to defend and protect everyone), and Timmy (who protects Carla through avoidance as an escape artist).

Carleen (notice that her name is a diminutive form of Carla) is related to Timmy because she is a child alter. Godiva is a negative alter, a persecutor, and is not connected to the rest.

NUMBERS OF ALTERS

The average number of alters in a multiple has increased over the years. Fifty or one hundred years ago, the cases reported two or three personalities. In more recent years, Dr. Frank Putnam's research on multiples found the average number of alters to be thirteen. Multiples have been reported with over one or two hundred personalities.[5]

> *The more alters a multiple has, the less likely they will exist as full personalities, and the less opportunity they will have to be disruptive.*

Multiples with more than one hundred personalities are referred to as *supermultiples.* However, they are not full personalities; most are personality *fragments* who came out to fill a one-time specific function. Supermultiples have undergone long-term abuse—from early childhood well into the teen years—that is believed to have been more severe.

The confusion in a multiple's life stems not from the *number* of alters but from the role or function the individual alters play. The more alters a multiple has, the less likely they will exist as full personalities, and the less opportunity they will have to be disruptive.

Having nineteen alter personalities does not mean that the person trades off nineteen times each day with each personality. Most of the alters are not out very often. Some may be inside for months at a time. Only a few are probably used regularly. For example, the multiple may frequently use the helper alter, the alter that holds the rage or handles anger, and the persecutor alter.

ALTERS IN RELATIONSHIP TO OTHER ALTERS

I have found that alters have a separate and unique relationship to the other alters.

1. *One-way amnesia* exists when alter number one knows about alter number two, but the second one does not know about the first one.

2. *Two-way amnesia* exists when neither alter knows about the other. Sometimes, these alters may sense that others are around, but it takes a while to find each other. If they are in therapy, the psychiatrist can help them to know about each other.

3. *Cocognizance* is the ability to know about the thoughts and behavior of the other alter personalities.

Most of the alters know about the multiple, but the core personality does not know about the alters (until the revelation is made, usually in therapy). However, the multiple hears the voices of the alters in her head, which is both puzzling and frightening. She hears the alters discussing her, arguing about her behavior and things of which she has no knowledge or memory.

The alters observe the multiple's behavior and know her feelings and attitudes, though they are unable to directly influence them. If the alters feel the host will do something they don't want, one of the alter personalities could switch in to physically prevent it. For instance, an alter will hide the razor blades a host or other alter has bought with suicidal intentions. Or in the case of Lorinda (in the first chapter), one of the alters could come into therapy or an emergency ward to prevent a suicide.

The alters often know about each other but not necessarily and not fully. They might be partially cognizant, meaning that some have an awareness of only some of the others or only some of the information and history of an alter.

Alters are not all friends, either. The personalities might mesh, complement one another, or be at odds with one another. Usually, the persecutor alter is feared by many because of the belligerent, angry, self-abusive, and self-destructive behavior. Likewise, the persecutor personality does not like the helper alter (seeing her as too much of a goody-goody who spoils all the fun) or the core personality (as too wimpy, a pushover, or depressive). Despite their differences, however, these alternate personalities will pull together in a second to exert a protective effect for themselves and/or the host personality if they believe someone on the outside will harm them in any way.

4. *Copresence* is the ability to *coexist* with another personality—sort of sharing the driver's seat! In this situation, the alters are cocognizant and are separate per-

sonalities who can confer back and forth and decide a course of action. Copresence usually happens before fusion or integration. Before the host reaches this stage with any of the alters, she can know about the alters only through her therapist.[6]

ALTERS IN RELATIONSHIP TO OTHER PEOPLE

People with MPD are for the most part highly functional individuals. They are in almost every profession you can imagine—from college professor to ballet dancer, from real estate broker to counselor.

Friends and spouses would describe them as moody or prone to getting into one of their states (depressed state, artistic state, etc.). Since the switch from one personality to another is usually very subtle, often friends and associates never see how marked the separate identities can be.

When a diagnosis is revealed, about half of those close to the person with MPD are relieved to find a logical explanation for some peculiarities they have observed. The other half are disbelieving! They find the concept of the diagnosis overwhelming and will typically say something like, "Oh, sure, you've always been overly dramatic, or you certainly have your moods—but multiple personalities?"

When a distinct personality occurs, such as Veronica Daniels, I have noted that this personality rarely pops out in day-to-day activities. These alters have separate friends who see them only in the settings appropriate to their character. I doubt that any of Veronica's clients ever came to LA to meet her on a surprise visit. She would meet them at upscale restaurants, galleries, and all the venues appropriate to her field. Then they wouldn't see her again for some time.

HOW DO THE ALTERS GET NAMED?

From my observation, alters get their names from one of three ways:

1. They say they are just "born" with that name. The alter comes into being with a name. That probably happens when the alter is named after a person, either real or fictional (e.g., Timmy from Busy Timmy). The mind has clearly modeled the alter after a character for a particular purpose and thus can supply the name automatically.

2. The alter has a particular emotional response, and the name developed from that behavior (e.g., the Sad One, Angry Janie).

3. The name is symbolic for the role of an alter within the multiple family system (e.g., Director was a helper personality who got everything organized and off the ground).

Incidentally, although each alter has a name, each knows to respond to the name of the birth personality. Male alter personalities believe themselves to be grown men (or teenagers) but know that they are somehow tied in with a woman figure and that people in the outside world will call them by her name. In cases like Veronica's, friends who are unique to one alter personality will unexpectedly run into "her" when the core personality is in control (in this case, Regina). These friends might say, "Veronica, I didn't expect to see you. I had no idea you would be here!" The multiple might say, "Oh, no, my name is Regina. You must be mistaken." The individual mannerisms, clothes, and speech might fool the friend into thinking it is a case of mistaken identity. On the other hand, if these incidents happen frequently enough, the multiple (who is already used to a life full of unexplained surprises) will go along with being called Veronica to hide that there is a problem. Once again, she will wonder vaguely, "Who are these people, and why do they know me? Why do they keep calling me by different names?"

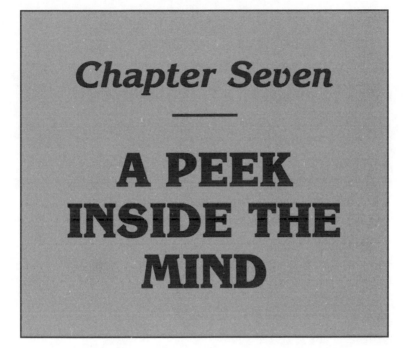

Chapter Seven

—

A PEEK INSIDE THE MIND

BEHIND THE SCREEN

We all live in a very beautiful garden that is behind a large silky white screen, like a huge gossamer scarf. There are rows of blue delphinium and larkspur, roses and lilies, camellias and carnations and Queen Anne's lace and all kinds of beautiful, beautiful flowers. Gardenias scent the air, and along the back and one side of the garden are fruit trees—orange and lemon and lime, apples and plums, and my favorite, nectarines.

"Some of us draw and paint landscapes, or we like to walk through the garden because it is so peaceful and beautiful. Usually, the children like to lie out on the grass and do watercolors. Sometimes we read books while sitting on rocks overlooking the valley below.

"If we walk up to the screen, to this big piece of white, white silk, we can see lights and hear sounds on the other side. It is like we are on the other side of the curtain in a play. If we want to be in that play, we go up to the little gate alongside of the edge of the white silk and wait for our turn. Usually, we just know when it is our time to go through the gate. Sometimes another person comes up to us and taps us on the shoulder and says it's time for us to come out. We can watch what goes on if we look beyond the gate. Sometimes a couple of us will just lean up against the gate and watch her, but she never sees us.''

One of the alters of a patient with multiple personality disorder gave me this description when I asked her to tell me where all of the personalities live and how they came out. I wanted to know what she did when she and the other alternate personalities were not out and what they thought about. I remain fascinated that the mind can do all this and essentially have a mind within a mind. Over the years, I have learned that each multiple has a unique internal world. Sometimes, it is orderly and organized; other times, the descriptions do not make sense, and I cannot compare them to anything I've experienced in this world.

> *Each multiple has a unique internal world.*

Dr. Ralph Allison, another psychiatrist who has a specialty in treating people with MPD, received the following insight from an alter of a multiple he was treating: "Doctor, you know there is an infinite physical world outside this body. Inside the mind there is an equally infinite world in which I live. Each of us in there perceives that world differently."[1]

A Peek Inside

For each of my multiple patients, there is a different inside world where they have their individual activities and amusements and hobbies, just as we would have on the outside. At any rate, they remain busy inside until it is their turn to come out and the process of switching occurs.

SWITCHING

When an alter comes out or exchanges places with another alter or the core personality, this action is called switching. Switching is usually sudden and is accompanied by subtle or not-so-subtle facial movements. My multiple patients have demonstrated this switching mechanism in several ways:

- Rolling their eyes up

- Lowering their head as though they are feeling weak

- Giving one gigantic and overexaggerated blink

- Simultaneously grimacing and blinking

You may be wondering, "How does an alter know when to switch in and take over the body? Is anything controlling the switching? Or what if everybody tries to come out at once?"

One alter personality works as the master switch and decides who should go in and out. I have found the rescuer personality is usually in control of this function. This personality is an adult and is the most logical and rational (relatively speaking) of the group. The rescuer acts like a decisive CEO and determines who is best suited for the job at hand.

THE SWITCHER

Most of the time, the rescuer will perform the switcher role and assign an alter to manage the crisis. For instance, if the multiple is in physical danger, the rescuer might call out an alter with great physical strength. For multiples involved in cults, probably several alters can handle different functions. However, I have also observed that there are times when an alter who really wants to be out will simply push herself out front somehow. They describe themselves as "watching" the proceedings and then determining they want to be part of the events.

Alters describe themselves as "watching" the proceedings and then determining they want to be part of the events.

Conversely, an alter may get herself in trouble and then dive inside, leaving the confused multiple not knowing why she is in a particular situation or what to do. Godiva did that constantly to Carla.

Godiva, if you'll remember, was a self-destructive and irresponsible alter. On the one hand, she could be delightfully fresh and silly and spontaneous. On the other hand, many of her other alters would become very angry with her for putting the rest of them at risk so many times. Godiva would go to dives and raunchy nightclubs. She would flit around giddily like a young teenager and pick up men. Then, at times as the men got Godiva home or would start to make a move on her, she would disappear!

At that point, the terrified Carla would wake up to find herself with a man she did not know, and she would have no idea where she was or how she got there. If the situation was particularly overwhelming, Carla would pass out, and another alter would have to come out to handle the situation.

Sometimes, C. J. (the big, burly male alter) would come out, punch the guy, and leave. In other episodes, Christine would enter to capably handle the situation with her no-nonsense logic and negotiation skills.

On at least one occasion, Timmy, the eight-year-old escape artist, was the personality pushed out into one of those scenarios. His job was to talk his way out of the situation. Suddenly finding himself with a person acting like a young grade-school boy was probably as shocking for the man as the experience with C. J.

SUMMARY

Although this mysterious disorder, full of surprises for the multiple and those around her, has been overlooked for many years, it is not a new problem that has evolved out of twentieth-century stresses. What is new is our understanding of it. Multiple personality disorder is one of the greatest testaments to the human survival instinct. It is the perfect internal defense to trauma for those who have to defend themselves from external trauma that they cannot prevent. In coming to understand this defense disorder, we must not overlook the intense pain that each person with MPD has experienced. The pain and its intensity can only be fully understood in the context of the origin of MPD. These roots almost always spring from an early childhood of severe abuse.

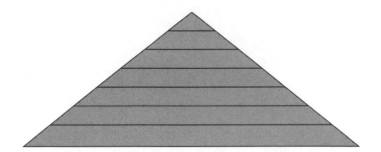

Section 2

ROOTS

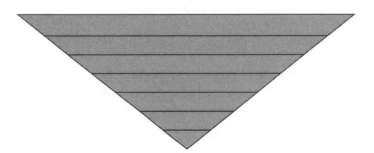

Chapter Eight

———

CHILD ABUSE AND MULTIPLE PERSONALITY DISORDER

CHARLENE'S STORY

Charlene was only two and a half years old when she first learned about trust. She was in her backyard, which consisted of a few trees and a small square of grass and dandelions surrounded by a sidewalk. She was exploring a ladybug on a long overgrown stalk of grass when her mother came through from the back screen door, sweeping out dirt in front of her. The mother had on a blue cotton shirtdress with a striped apron. Her dark brown hair was short and wavy and thick, just like her daughter Charlene's. The mother caught sight of Charlene and came forward to join her. She swooped Charlene up and put her on a thick branch of one of the big fruit trees.

"Want to play, honey?" her mother asked. "Jump into my arms, Charlene! Mommy will catch you! You can do it! Come on now. Jump!" Charlene looked down at the lanky outstretched arms of her mother. "Don't be afraid, Mommy can catch you!" her mother called out.

Charlene stepped forward and jumped. Her mother stepped back and away to the side. Charlene still remembers her mother's laugh as her face slammed into the ground. This was a lesson in trust—"Don't trust." The incident ripped away any and all ability to ever trust an adult.

Charlene was three months shy of her sixth birthday when she learned about not loving.

She had a small brown terrier named Taffy that she absolutely adored. He had been a present from a neighbor with too many pups. Taffy was Charlene's best friend. She had no one else to play with. She had no brothers and sisters, and her father had moved away. But Taffy could be her friend.

Charlene often would run around in circles in the tiny backyard with Taffy racing along with her, yapping at her heels. Then Charlene would collapse, breathless and sweaty, into the tall sweet grass while Taffy danced dizzily around her and yelped for more action.

Sometimes, Charlene would try to put one of her doll bonnets on Taffy's head, which he would shake off with annoyance. She loved to have him sleep at the end of her bed, right between her feet and the footboard, and then be awakened by his little pink tongue licking at her face in the morning.

One Sunday, Charlene's father drove her back from her grandmother's house after she had spent the weekend there with her dad. As she came through the front door, she was surprised that Taffy was not there to jump up and greet her.

Charlene's mother came out from the kitchen after her ex-husband left. Charlene gave her mother a quick hug, then asked, "Mom, where's Taffy? I haven't seen him, have you? I missed him so much."

"You spend too much time with that dog, Charlene. You mustn't care so much about anything."

"Mommy! I just want to play with him. Do you know where he is?" Charlene peered out the back door. "Taffy! Here, Taffy! Taffy, come here! Where is he, Mommy? I can't find him anywhere," she cried.

Charlene never saw Taffy alive again. Her mother sternly lectured that she should never love anyone or anything so much.

"Charlene, you don't need that dog anymore. You need to play with new things." With that, Charlene's mother threw her head back and gave another of her long laughs.

Charlene learned that it was not safe to love.

Charlene was twenty-six when her gynecologist told her that she could never bear children. Charlene had no idea how the scar tissue was formed in her uterus or why there were scars on her vagina. As a four-year-old, she was not the personality present when her mother physically abused her.

By that time, she had already developed three other alternate personalities to handle shock and pain.

Charlene was thirty-three years old when I began to see her in my office. As we uncovered her stories, my heart went out to the young child who lived in such a cold and bewildering world that made no sense. My heart grieved for the little girl who was never allowed to learn normal and healthy emotions. My heart ached at the thought of the young girl raised in this home full of pain and disappointment.

CHILD ABUSE

Nowhere are the effects of child abuse more dramatically revealed than in a patient with MPD. With relatively few exceptions, MPD finds its roots in extreme and unrelenting child abuse, and that often is delivered in the form of satanic ritual abuse. Studies show that child abuse is the cause of 97 percent of cases of multiple personality disorder.[1] Extreme physical abuse and sexual abuse damage the child physically, emotionally, and spiritually.

> *With relatively few exceptions, MPD finds its roots in extreme and unrelenting child abuse, and that often is delivered in the form of satanic ritual abuse.*

In very early childhood, it is difficult for the child to integrate body, mind, willpower, and feelings. At that stage, the child is vulnerable to the experiences of dissociation. In multiples, the average age is about four when the first dissociative experience takes place. Experts theorize that if the child goes through too many experiences of dissociation that are positively enforced (with the successful temporary avoidance of pain), the child will not learn to coordinate and integrate these components of personality. Instead, these components will remain compartmentalized through the child's experiences of dissociation. One personality will handle one experience; another alter will handle a different emotion. Nobody (certainly not the multiple) knows or remembers what everybody else has been doing.

The most common perpetrators of this level of abuse are the parents and/or stepparents. Secondary perpetrators include grandparents and extended family members. Rarely does the abuse of a person with MPD come from outside the extended family. The repeated abuse from an authority figure calls for a system of extensive and close contact.

Some cases of MPD were a result of emotional or psychological abuse rather than sexual or physical abuse. Along with these acts come constant criticism and insults that rob the child of a healthy self-image. These parents go out of their way to set up situations to disappoint, humiliate, or frighten the child. When the psychological terror becomes too intense to bear, the child dissociates and splits off into a newly created personality that will often have characteristics destroyed from abuse to the core personality.

Emotional abuse can also take on the form of emotional incest. A child is born into a troubled marriage and becomes the complete focus of one parent's life, usually the one of the opposite sex. As the child grows older, the relationship between parent and child becomes more significant than the relationship between the two parents. Gradually, the child takes on the role of spouse, leaving one spouse completely out of the relationship. This type of emotional abuse is perplexing and devastating for the child. She feels pulled into it by her own need for attention, but the attention obtained from one parent is unhealthy and the same-sex parent may be angry and jealous of the child.

PHYSICAL ABUSE

Most people are unaware of just how horrible physical abuse can be for children. The sickest among us are able to deliver torture beyond what most people can imagine. This bizarre delivery of physical pain goes far beyond an overwrought parent who slaps or whips a child.

Much of the child abuse in the lives of people with MPD is absolute sadism. The cases I have dealt with include stories of parents and/or stepparents, grandparents, and even day-care providers

- purposely shocking children with electrical equipment.

- burning children with cigarettes.

- holding down children's hands over the stove, an iron, an open flame, a waffle iron, a heater or heat register.

- holding the child upside down and immersing the head in water (in a filled kitchen sink, a toilet, or a well).

- partially suffocating children (waiting until they pass out).

- forcing the child to sit or stand in an area full of spiders.

- putting the child in a box or small confined quarters and then throwing in live snakes or rodents on top of the terrified child.

• locking up the child in a trunk, box, closet, or refrigeration compartment.

Some children are tortured so regularly that they come to expect it as a commonplace occurrence and

> *Some children are tortured so regularly that they come to expect it as a commonplace occurrence and will help the parent prepare for the "ritual."*

will help the parent prepare for the "ritual." One little child would put a towel on the floor next to the wall so that when her father finished beating her and knocking her against the wall, she would not bleed on the carpet. These stories should cause all of us to have deep compassion for the survivors of such abuse.

SEXUAL ABUSE

Sexual abuse transcends the degradation of physical abuse because it is a more intimate and, therefore, a more personal violation. This form of abuse strikes at the very core of the personality and can disrupt the soul, the psyche, and the spirit of the child. No wonder the Bible has described sexual relations with another person as "knowing" another person. Something unique about sexual relations taps into the spirit and the very essence of who we are. Unwanted and unwilling sexual experiences rob individuals of the ability to protect their ego center and their personhood.

An incomplete portrait of sexual abuse would highlight father-daughter incest. But as is the case with non-sexual physical abuse, much more is involved than that stereotype. In my work with patients with MPD, I have seen just as many mothers guilty of sexually abusing their daughters and sons. In my work with patients who have been involved with satanic cults, I have seen that both parents subjected their daughters to regular rapings and tortures by other cult members.

Parents subject their children to sexual abuse in other ways. Much of it doesn't involve touching, such as showing children X-rated movies or having them watch sexual acts. Whatever the form, the cruelty and effects of the experience cannot be overestimated. Few events more completely abort a person's chance for a healthy life than repeated sexual violation.

RITUAL ABUSE

As we approach the end of the twentieth century, we in our open and honest American society have prided ourselves to think we've been able to uncover, inspect, and discuss just about every taboo topic and controversial subject there is. However, the last closet door has only begun to be cracked open. I am talking about underground satanic cult abuse, which has increasingly been noted by the mental health community as well as the law enforcement field. Although the subject of satanic ritual abuse (SRA as it is known in the psychiatric and law enforcement communities) will be discussed in more detail in Section 3, I wish to mention the range of abuses in this category as it pertains to MPD.

Briefly, these rituals involve the systematic abuse—psychological and physical—of people of all ages. The terrorizing of very young children continues through preadolescence. It provides sadistic pleasure for the older cult members as well as the opportunity to purposefully create MPD within some of the children. The goal is to produce alter personalities that will respond or perform on cue to the demands of the cult officials.

Initially, these children (whose parents or grandparents or other relatives or caretakers are members of the cult) are psychologically abused and terrorized. They are regularly forced to watch other children or adults being tortured or raped.

Girls—as young as two or three years old—are strapped to altars and must endure being stripped and inspected by cult members, a practice that further humiliates and depersonalizes them.

Children are buried alive in small coffins and covered with dirt, spiders, and worms, which is extraordinarily traumatizing and psychologically terrifying.[2] Usually, the high priest or other cult leader will rescue them so the children are forced to think of the perpetrator as a rescuer and savior.

A common event is the decapitation or mutilation of a small animal, such as a cat or rabbit. The children are then forced to touch the animal. A cult member closes this ritual with a demand that the children swear to secrecy lest the same event befall them.

THEORIES OR CAUSES OF MPD

In a discussion of MPD, many questions have yet to be answered. There are no definitively known causes or proven origins for the disorder. However, many theories attempt to provide explanations and understanding of factors leading to MPD. As academic interest and research in the disorder increase, many other mysteries of the inner workings of the mind are certain to be uncovered along the way to sorting out the pieces to the puzzle of MPD.

Physiological Theories

Some of the research surrounding MPD has indicated that there may be, at least in part, a biological or hereditary component for the disorder. These researchers are looking for physiological factors that may be missing or may be more predominant in multiples. Given the similarities in the stories of abuse, I find little reason to believe genetics alone lay the foundation for this disorder.

The rationale for this approach is this: child abuse affects thousands of children annually, but not all of the children who survive it develop multiple personalities. The genetic research focuses on what qualities or factors determine whether a child will develop multiple personalities. Researchers are now trying to look at variables of genetics such as intelligence and creativity to determine how they may play a part in MPD.

The ability early on to dissociate is the most significant factor in this disorder. Multiples are highly hypno-tizable, and hypnosis is a dissociated state. Is this ability to dissociate genetically determined, or is it a talent that can be developed with practice? To put it another way, the question researchers are trying to decide is: Do these children dissociate and then improve on this tech-nique over the course of their lives so that it develops to a finely honed skill? Or is this ability to dissociate already a prodigious talent in toddlers that has allowed them to survive as multiples?

In compiling family histories for patients with MPD, researchers have determined that other family members (besides siblings) may have been, or in fact were, also multiple personality.[3]

Psychodynamic Theories

MPD is strongly tied in with disordered family dynam-ics and relationships. Like child abuse, the disorder can occur in any family, regardless of race, religion, educa-tion, or income. A significantly or severely dysfunctional family is part of the history of almost every person with MPD, however.

In the dysfunctional family system, there is always a two-sided component. On one side is the real problem, and on the other side is the reactive problem. The real problem is the original problem or trauma that causes each family member to react in an unhealthy way. Per-haps a parent or main caretaker has a problem with drugs or alcoholism. In many multiples' families, we see strong evidence for a significant psychiatric problem, such as schizophrenia or one parent could have MPD.

The other half of the problem is the reactive problem.

> *Like child abuse, MPD can oc-cur in any family, regardless of race, religion, education, or income.*

One might suppose that the rest of the family or at least the spouse would come forward and confront the problem (drugs, mental illness, or the person). One might think that the family would react with outrage and/or concern and decisively deal with the problem. Instead, nothing happens. The family dynamics or interpersonal relationships are disturbed. The disturbance is not discussed. Communication is restricted. Each member is left on his or her own to cope and to develop survival skills in the absence of freedom to talk about the problem or express hurt over it.

When the problem continues, when it is not acknowledged or talked about, other family members are deceived into believing there is no problem. The child thinks to herself, *If nobody is doing anything about this, and nobody is even talking about this, maybe there is not really a problem! Maybe nothing is wrong, and I shouldn't have these feelings.* The next seemingly logical conclusion often drawn by the child is that *there is something wrong, but since no one seems to see it or is talking about it to me, I must be the problem.*

Another characteristic of the families of those with MPD is rigidity. The families seem to have extremely narrow views; everything is very much black or white for one parent or a significant caregiver. They are often overinvolved in highly legalistic churches. Most view God as fearsome, angry, and vengeful. Punishment and suffering are necessary to atone for sins or mistakes. In these homes, religious rules and narrow codes of behavior replace a relationship with a loving God and benevolent heavenly Father, as well as the power of the saving grace of Jesus Christ.

The homes in which my patients grew up were intense and driven, but life was unpredictable. In this setting, confusion is created where the young child never knows what is expected. Arbitrary punishment prevents the child from learning the cause and effect relationship between behavior and consequences. The members of her family are not "safe." It is not safe to love or trust. Doing good things can be bad; doing bad things can be good.

Demonic Possession

Demonic possession in many ways can mimic MPD, but they are two separate issues. People with MPD are *not* possessed by demons, nor have their bodies been taken over by evil spirits as in the fictional book and movie *The Exorcist.* We do a grave injustice to these patients and add confusion, fear, and shame to their very real injuries by telling them that they are controlled by demons.

Telling a multiple that the problem is possession can very likely worsen the problem because an alter may become frightened at the prospect of being demonic and go into hiding. A well-hidden or deeply buried alter can be very difficult to uncover in therapy and may prolong the healing process.

This is not to say that a person could not have MPD and be possessed by an evil spirit. Certainly, possession is a possibility if a person has been involved to any degree in underground satanic cults. However, the manifested disorder of multiple personalities, in and of itself, does not indicate possession or control by an outside spirit or other entity.

Integrated Theory

Dr. Richard Kluft is a psychiatrist who has worked with multiple personalities and has done extensive research on MPD and children. Kluft has proposed a four-factor theory for the development of MPD that integrates aspects from environment and heredity. He believes that all four components are necessary for the onset of multiple personality disorder:[4]

1. A biological capacity for dissociation
> This refers to the physiological nature of dissociation.

2. A history of trauma or abuse
> Ritualistic, repeated child abuse is the predominant factor in MPD. Nearly 97 percent of all multiple patients have a history of child abuse lasting from four to fourteen years. It starts early—between the ages of two and four—and involves physical, sexual, emotional, and/or psychological abuse. It is ongoing and unrelenting. The

home life offers the child no real opportunity for escape, comfort, or respite from any of the pain.

3. Specific psychological structure or contents that can be used in the creation of alternate personalities

Throughout the literature and research done on the subject, multiple personalities have been identified as extraordinarily gifted individuals— bright, talented, and creative. When multiples are given IQ tests, they generally score in the above average range and are considered to be in the gifted through genius ranges of intelligence. Multiples are unusually perceptive and artistic— and excel as painters, illustrators, and poets.[5]

All of these attributes appear to be critical in light of what we observe that the mind accomplishes in MPD. This disorder requires an exceptional capacity—such as an intelligent and creative mind to produce the alter personalities and to organize their structure and behavior.

4. A lack of adequate nurturing or opportunities to recover from abuse

The inability to escape seems to be the most critical factor that forces the mind to split into multiple personalities. The child is isolated and alone, trapped with no way out and no one to rescue or help her. Fragmentation is the only respite from the pain and confusion. It is most disturbing to consider the plight of the child.

Looking back on my own childhood, I remember playing various games and sports. Sometimes, the activity would get to such a frenzied pace that we were all out of breath physically or out of ideas on how to head off the other team, or someone had fallen and gotten hurt in the process of the game. Regardless of the case, someone [a caretaker] would call a time out, and we could regroup. We could catch our breath after all the running, stop to help our fallen teammate, or pause to think about the best strategic plan to get ourselves ahead or get the other team out of the way.

The time out is the one element that could save a child who is growing up in the abusive situations described in MPD. Unfortunately, outside the fragmentation, this opportunity to catch her breath, to regroup, to test her feelings against fact, or to receive compassion and comfort and have a safe place to go, does not seem to come. There is no safe person to turn to.

SUMMARY

What is common in each person with MPD are roots of extreme pain from abuse. This pain is so intense that it cannot be endured alone. The mind of the person with MPD uses all of its capacities to survive the suffering and confusion that goes on around the person.

Commonly, the people we see who have developed MPD have a capacity to dissociate to a great extent. We believe that family members, including parents, also have this capacity. There may be a genetic correlate to their ability to dissociate in this way and to the extent exhibited by the patients. Commonly, we see other exceptional capabilities such as creativity, perceptivity, and above average intelligence.

The types of abuse we see vary from severe psychological abuse to physical, sexual, and emotional abuse. The abuse is repeated and long-term, beginning in early childhood, and the child has no place to go for relief and no one to trust. The child finds the only respite from pain is fragmentation of the mind and disowning of the events and pain of his or her life.

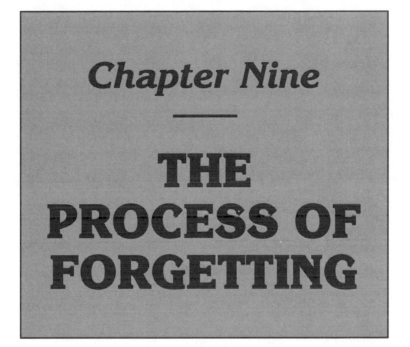

Chapter Nine

THE PROCESS OF FORGETTING

REGINA REMEMBERS

When the personality of Veronica Daniels came to Regina's appointment, she told me that Regina was taking a few days off for a mental health holiday. Regina had been overstressed and overworked by a twelve-hour-a-day schedule for nearly three weeks straight. Her company was shooting and editing a documentary and was operating under a demanding time schedule. Since our regular appointments were on Wednesday afternoons, Regina's break would essentially be a pleasant five-day holiday. I asked Veronica what her immediate plans were for that holiday. She intended to go to Santa Barbara to check out a few antique stores and to pick up two botanical prints at a fine print gallery in the old Paseo area downtown.

I was intrigued to determine how this could all work out and curious to find out what would take place over the next several days and who would be in charge. I wanted to know if Veronica would make it to Santa Barbara, or would Regina stay in Van Nuys and rest? I wondered if another alter personality with a different agenda for either rest or recreation might take over and lead the group in another direction.

When Regina was back for her regular appointment, she came in wearing stylishly baggy beige pants with a long-sleeved green silk blouse and a French-style scarf around her neck. She was already deeply involved in a new project, an educational video series for a major school district. However, I noticed that she seemed more assertive and aggressive rather than stressed and frazzled.

As we settled down to get into the heart of the session, I expressed to her how glad I was that she was able to take some time off to get much-needed rest. I asked her if she did anything special or went anyplace during her short holiday. She looked lost in thought for a second, then shrugged her shoulders, and looked down.

"No . . . nothing really. Just the usual stuff. You know—cleaning and straightening up. Nothing interesting," she said.

I decided to push a little to see how far I could go.

"Well, I *am* interested. You've been working brutal hours for so long. I hope that you were able to do something nice for yourself . . . something far more pleasant than just cleaning house for five days! You deserved some kind of fun activity. Did you see any new movies? Did you go out of town?"

Regina shifted. Did I sense that she looked uncomfortable?

"No, nothing really. I can't really think of anything much that I did. Just hung around. . . . Nothing really too exciting, like I said."

I decided to fish a little more. "Well, I know the feeling, Regina. Sometimes the best thing is to take it easy. Stay around the house or just go window shopping at the mall. Did you get a chance to do anything like that? Maybe buy some clothes? Or did you get those botanical prints?"

When I asked about the prints, I landed on a spark that ignited her curiosity.

Regina's expression was one of surprise and dismay and pain, all at the same time. "Yes, well, yes . . . how did you . . . did I tell you that already? I . . . sometimes I just lose all track of time or whatever. You know, I'm forgetful." She was flustered.

"I was wondering if you got the prints from Santa Barbara you were talking about at a previous session," I offered.

"Yes. Yes, they were from Santa Barbara. . . . I saw the bag. Did I already say anything about the flower prints? . . . Gosh . . . I guess I forgot about that."

Okay, so I knew that she was in Santa Barbara. Or I was willing to bet that Veronica got her chance to go there.

"So, how was Santa Barbara?" I asked innocently. "You know my undergraduate years were at UCSB, and I remember what a pretty place it was."

"It was nice, yeah. . . ." Her voice trailed off.

"Regina." It was a command. "Tell me something. It's important for me to know. Do you specifically remember anything about your trip to Santa Barbara? Can you remember driving up? Do you remember going to the gallery and picking out your prints?"

Silence.

"No." A huge sigh. "I guess not really."

"When did you know about going to Santa Barbara?

When you saw the prints in the bag with the name of the store and the city?"

"Yes. . . . I found it on the side table in my living room. Sometimes I guess I forget the most obvious things. . . . I just don't know how to explain it. I suppose I'm afraid maybe I've got some form of Alzheimer's or something. I just have blank spells. I can't remember. I guess I'm too forgetful or something."

"Most of your time off over these past few days was a kind of 'blank spell' as you described it, wasn't it, Regina? You have no clear memory of what you were doing, right?" I said in what I hoped was a helpful, encouraging way.

"Yes."

"Regina, I'll bet sometimes you find clues around the house that jog your memory and remind you of what you might have been doing during your blank spells, as you call them. The bag from Santa Barbara was one clue. Do you sometimes find clothes in your closet that you don't remember shopping for?"

"Yes." She seemed a bit relieved.

"Do people often tell you about things you said or did that you don't remember?"

"Yes. That happens. . . . I can't explain how. I just don't know about these things or how they happen. I guess somehow I just forget about stuff before I even have a chance to remember it the first time."

DISSOCIATION AND FORGETTING

Dissociation is all about forgetting. *Suppression* may be a matter of trying not to think about something, but dissociation is (as Regina so aptly stated) forgetting before you even have a chance to remember. It is the ultimate in denial in the sense that the body says, "This event is not even happening to me." But the memory is held in the conscious awareness of some facet of the mind.

Confronted with unrelenting abuse, a child may turn to dissociation as the only means of survival. The little child says to herself, "I'm not feeling hurt, and I don't feel pain because I don't know anything about this." She can forget before she remembers because somebody else—another alter—is the one who will have to remember. This other alter will hold the memory of these events and will remember the emotion and pain that accompanied it.

That explains the disjointedness of the disorder. Multiples do not know what is going on in their lives. Regina could not remember going to Santa Barbara because she didn't. *Veronica* went to Santa Barbara, visited the galleries, and did some shopping. Veronica will remember everything that she did, but Regina can't remember what didn't happen to her. The separate experiences of each alter are locked in the separate memory banks of each alter.

DISSOCIATION AND AMNESIA

Whenever an alter is out and in control, collecting memories and experiences, the birth personality is amnesiac for what has taken place. She remembers nothing! There will be a big hole in her memory that she will describe as a blank spell or a blackout or missing time. She will remember whatever was happening to her right up until the point of another alter switching out. As soon as that alter switches back in, and she comes out, the memory trace will pick up again.

In the process of switching the brain, the emotions, the memories, and the physical body "disconnect" from what is happening.

When something is disconnected, there are two pieces rather than one. In MPD, the disconnection results in two people. That is why a multiple will not remember her childhood—the body, mind, and spirit were completely disconnected from the core personality during the time she was experiencing abuse. If the abuse did not happen to her, she is unable to remember anything about it. However, if you were to ask one of the alter personalities, you would likely get a much different response. He or she would obviously know a lot more about what happened.

> *The disconnection phenomenon can become so intense that multiples will describe out-of-body experiences.*

The disconnection phenomenon can become so intense that multiples will describe out-of-body experiences. They seem very similar to the out-of-body experiences described by persons undergoing near-death experiences. The most common type of out-of-body experience for multiples is one in which the multiple senses that she is above her body, looking down on herself while abuse is taking place.

NORMAL DISSOCIATIONS

Dissociation in and of itself does not cause disruption and confusion for the person with MPD. The combination of dissociation with amnesia and the alter personalities creates the disorder. Dissociation by itself is a normal process that most of us use to some degree throughout our lives. It is neither unnatural nor unhealthy.

For instance, when I attended the University of California at Santa Barbara, I had about a two-hour drive back to my parents' home in Los Angeles. Traffic in Los Angeles is much different from that in most of the rest of the state. Almost anywhere you go in Los Angeles requires a freeway, and they are six- or eight-lane freeways. With several million cars added in, you can just about bet on stop-and-go traffic—plus at least one accident a day to slow down traffic.

When I was in Santa Barbara, even in rush-hour traffic, the freeway barely slowed down—and there were only two lanes in each direction. I loved the drive home to LA every couple of weeks or so because the freeway went alongside or near the coast through most of Santa Barbara and Ventura counties before entering Los Angeles. The drive was very easy—it was not stop-and-go heavy traffic, and I didn't have to be on my guard every second. I never had to dodge other cars or brake every sixty yards. However, it also became too easy to become lost in thought. With the beautiful Pacific on my right, mountains on my left, and no traffic to speak of, I was deep in thought about a hundred different things. Sometimes I would enter Ventura and suddenly realize that I had absolutely no recollection of having passed the Rincon area. Other times I would head into Thousand Oaks and find that I could not remember going up the Conejo Grade!

That is dissociation.

Dissociation can occur when we are so lost in the plot of a novel that we do not hear our friends or family when they call us. Dissociation happens to every teenage girl who daydreams in class about some boy she has a crush on and tunes out the teacher's lecture. Dissociation is in operation when an individual is under hypnosis.

These forms and examples of dissociation are everyday occurrences and do not indicate anything of a disorder or dysfunction. These dissociations are temporary disconnections from the real world, and as you will notice, they all involve amnesia. When we dissociate, we do not remember what is taking place in the real world because the events in our minds become disconnected. Because our minds disconnect from what we are dealing with, we do not know and cannot remember what is taking place and our minds are on something else.

Psychogenic Fugue

We all have moments when stress or worry from work or school seems to overtake us. For some individuals, when that pressure becomes overwhelming and then is compounded by drugs and/or depressing emotional

> *Because our minds disconnect from what we are dealing with, we do not know and cannot remember what is taking place and our minds are on something else.*

problems (marital strife, loss of job, etc.), the result can be psychogenic fugue.

We get the word *fugue* from *flight,* and that is exactly what happens. The persons will literally take flight to leave the situation and escape. In layperson's terms, I might describe it as a brain being on overload and about to blow, so the system shuts down. Typically, for a few hours or days, individuals will drive out of town or to another location until the mind has a chance to recover from the confusion. During this flight, they don't remember who they are or where they are going or what they should be doing. Sometimes, they take on a new identity or personality. Afterward, they have no memory of what they were doing during that time.

Psychogenic fugue is transient in nature and rare. It is not likely to occur more than once in an individual's lifetime. It is not permanent or chronic, nor will it become a regular pattern of behavior. A related disorder is psychogenic amnesia. It has just about the same purpose and nature of the psychogenic fugue, except that there is no flight. The individual will walk around in a fog, not remembering who he is or where he is or what he should be doing. Instead of a purposeful flight, there is an unpurposeful wandering. Psychogenic amnesia is more commonly aligned with natural disasters or war situations. Both involve a profound conflict or stressful situation.

While these amnesic conditions involve dissociation also, their pattern is very different from what we see in MPD. MPD is more common than both, and the amnesia experienced resides primarily in the birth personality with the memories being contained in the awareness of the alter personalities. Amnesia of MPD is episodic and recurrent and reoccurs over a long period of time.

SUMMARY

Amnesia for events, especially one's childhood, is a common finding in MPD. It is the result of the fragmentation that takes place to defend against the pain of the past. Persons with MPD are likely to have objects in their possession they cannot account for, or knowledge or skills they possess but do not remember how they acquired, or the absence of knowledge or skills that they should have but cannot tell you why they are lost. At a time when they feel safe, they will admit to a loss of continuity, time loss, and blanks or periods of blackouts.

Most multiples come to an awareness of some degree of the problem through their uneasiness about not being able to remember major chunks of their childhood and small pieces of a very confusing yesterday. Their minds have become masters at forgetting. This ability to forget provides a way out, a way to sustain life until someone provides hope for another way out. The memories are all there; they are in different compartments without a common corridor or links. The healing process involves unlocking each compartment and constructing pathways that can allow these memories to connect and form an integrated way of knowledge called the past of persons with MPD.

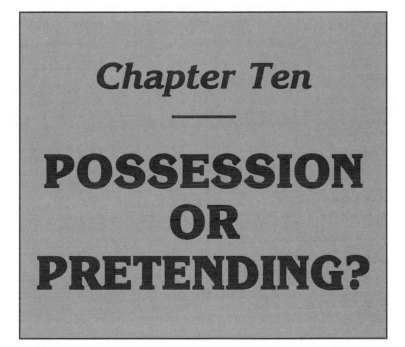

Chapter Ten

———

POSSESSION
OR
PRETENDING?

SKEPTICISM

After the American Psychiatric Association included multiple personality disorder in its *Diagnostic and Statistical Manual of Mental Disorders* in 1980, the door was opened toward clinical acceptance and understanding of the disorder. Yet we still have a long way to go.

Most persons in the mental health community at this point believe that if MPD does exist, it is a very, very rare thing that they will probably never encounter. This belief can be dangerous because it means that the therapists are not open to the possibility of accurately assessing or diagnosing MPD. They may miss or skip over a diagnosis of the disorder because they don't think they would ever have a patient with the problem. That is why the mental health community, which includes psychiatrists, psychologists, psychoanalysts, marriage and family counselors, and social workers, must understand the prevalence and scope of the disorder. A little ignorance can sentence a person with MPD to a life of disjointed reality.

More dangerous than therapists who perceive it as an extremely rare disorder are those who do not believe it

139

exists at all. In this group, we find two extremes. On one extreme, we find mental health care professionals who believe that the patients are faking it. They are convinced that these patients have latched onto a title—multiple personality disorder—and description and are acting out and pretending to be different personalities. They would say these patients are skillful actors and manipulative personalities who are feigning a disorder to avoid some other duty or responsibility and are pulling a fast one on the medical community and their families.

On the other extreme, we find those who believe that the behavior manifested by the multiple is real enough, but that it originates from possession—by a demon or evil spirit. The professionals in this arena are well-meaning but misguided. Some laypersons may be involved in pastoral counseling or as church paratherapists. Nonetheless, they see the alter personalities as separate entities, demonic in nature, that must be exorcised to be relieved as symptoms. They would hold that MPD is not a mental disorder but a problem of spirituality. While not discounting the impact of evil or the possibility of possession, this approach is not helpful to a person with MPD.

Both extreme views hold elements of truth, yet they are harmful in terms of helping a multiple come to grips with a very real and painful disorder. Neither view will heal the multiple and, in fact, can cause further damage.

PRETENDING

Some persons suggest that individuals are faking MPD to get attention or perhaps to make some gain for themselves through the exposure of the media. In consideration of the media coverage surrounding aspects of MPD, that might seem a possibility at first glance. For instance, when *Sybil* first was published in 1973, a tremendous amount was written up and reviewed about the book.

Not long after, in 1975, the infamous "Hillside Strangler" Kenneth Bianchi was brought to trial in Los Angeles for the rape and murder of thirteen girls. He claimed he was not guilty by reason of insanity because he had MPD. Three expert witnesses were brought in to assess whether he was a multiple. As it ended up, all three disagreed about that diagnosis. One thought he had MPD, another expert witness believed he had a related dissociative disorder as a result of his psychiatric evaluations, and still another believed that Bianchi was a clever fake.

During the 1980s, the media directed attention to the trial of Billy Milligan, a young man accused of rape in Ohio. As a young boy, Billy was severely sexually abused and tortured by his stepfather. The defense maintained that Billy Milligan had MPD, and that one of his alters committed the rape.

Because the legal system does not have an adequate avenue to deal with the unique aspects of MPD, again the defense was pleading innocent by reason of insanity. Billy was convicted but not before a great deal of publicity had gone out about his disorder and a great deal of discussion was held on whether he was faking all of his personalities.

During the 1990s, the media focused on a rape trial in Wisconsin. The jury had to decide whether a woman claiming to be a multiple was sexually assaulted. The debate lay in the fact that although one alter may have given the man consensual agreement, the man was told beforehand that the woman had a mentally handicapping condition and was vulnerable. It is a crime in Wisconsin to have sexual intercourse with a person believed to be mentally ill. The man was convicted of second degree assault.[1]

EVIDENCE

No wonder that John Barry, director of the Commission on the Mentally Disabled of the American Bar Association, had to concede that among those in the legal system "there's a great deal of disbelief about this disorder, a concern that people are faking."

To these and other disbelievers, I want to provide some major considerations about aspects of MPD.

The first aspect is behavioral. For those of us who have worked closely with multiples, we know that far from being attention seekers and publicity hounds, multiples go to great lengths to hide their disorder.

The second aspect is family history. The fact that somebody can brilliantly playact several personalities is not an indication of MPD. Although it may be true that a diagnosis of MPD may be confirmed with the presence of another alternate personality, the true alters do not appear in isolation of a traumatic childhood history as well as at least one or two of the other significant symptoms, such as amnesia, headaches, and blank spells.

The third, and most convincing, aspect deals with tangible physiological evidence. A clever actor cannot simulate changes in physiology. Researchers have been able to demonstrate verifiable differences among alters in

> *Multiples go to great lengths to hide their disorder.*

their heart rates, visual acuity, allergies, PET scans, voice prints, and visual field size.[2]

This disorder needs to gain understanding and acceptance from all of the mental health community because many of the treatments for other (misdiagnosed) disorders can be harmful to the multiple. If a psychiatrist thinks that she is treating a person with schizophrenia and prescribes the wrong treatment, the result can be disastrous for the multiple, who further splits and switches.

POSSESSION

Like Lorinda and MPD, the reality of demonic possession also came to me during my clinical experience as a psychiatrist. Over the course of my eight years in private practice I have confronted it on more than a few occasions.

On one such occasion the reality of demon possession became evident to our clinical team in one of the New Life Treatment Centers. New Life often works with multiples, so the initial consideration was that the display of bizarre behavior was the result of an alter personality, most likely the persecutor, taking control of a patient.

> *If a psychiatrist thinks that she is treating a person with schizophrenia and prescribes the wrong treatment, the result can be disastrous for the multiple, who further splits and switches.*

When it was over, all of us knew we had seen something very different.

For the first few days, the staff observed a distant and aloof female isolate herself from the rest of the patients. She interacted very little and seemed to be suspicious of everyone. The team knew it would take a while for her to feel comfortable enough to trust and open up about problems and pain.

One afternoon as other patients were preparing to eat dinner, a loud noise came from her room. When the nurse rushed in, she saw an overturned table, and the young female was sprawled out on the floor as if she were writhing in pain. As others entered the room, they observed her as she cursed the nurse with every vile name imaginable. She spewed forth a bitter tirade of hatred and anger that none of those watching could believe was coming from the previously quiet though detached woman.

They watched her for about five minutes before the chaplain entered the room with a Bible. The girl, in a very harsh male tone, demanded the chaplain leave. She shrieked an animal-like yell as she ordered him from the room. He persisted and went toward her and grabbed her hands and reassured her it would be okay. He was calm and gentle and told her not to worry, that it would be over soon. After several minutes she was calm and relaxed, showing signs of embarrassment over the outbursts and the attention she brought. After the chaplain left the room, he told the other staff he felt he had witnessed the presence of something from another world. No one on the staff had a hard time agreeing with him.

The incident points out the other area of concern in regard to possession and MPD.

BIBLICAL PERSPECTIVE

The scientific community often has trouble committing to anything that cannot be explained and validated by laboratory evidence. Although the laboratory cannot prove or disprove demon possession, plenty of empirical information should verify for most skeptics that possession of the body by an evil spirit continues to take place today.

At the same time, we must be extraordinarily careful about assuming anyone with MPD is possessed. That mistake is made often by many well-meaning Christian psychologists and psychiatrists who hold exorcisms for spirits that don't exist, frighten and confuse the alters, and demoralize the core personality in the process.

I can understand where the confusion or misunderstandings come from. Some aspects of the disorder no

> *Many well-meaning Christian psychologists and psychiatrists hold exorcisms for spirits that don't exist, frighten and confuse the alters, and demoralize the core personality in the process.*

doubt appear at first glance to resemble possession. Certainly, the persecutor alter, whose character is so unlike the core personality, could be a candidate for an evil entity. The persecutor has a slightly different voice from the core personality and often uses foul, angry language. The persecutor also engages in harmful, abusive, and self-destructive behavior. So, to the unknowledgeable, this alter could be a demon who took over the body of the otherwise meek and quiet core personality.

In general, I find several distinct differences between an alter and a demon. An alter is a personality; it can hold a rational conversation and can form relationships. An alter has a character. Even the persecutor alter, with all of its negative and self-destructive behavior, has unique interests, likes and dislikes, and idiosyncrasies. A demon has no such personality and forms no relationships; it has no personal characteristics. It is a negative voice that brings on guilt, shame, fear, hopelessness, and discouragement. Even the most disruptive persecutor does not try to alter the emotional disposition of the others in such a manner. Although an alter can experience any of those feelings and emotions, it remains independent from the other alters.

Jim Friesen, a Christian psychologist who has dealt with multiples, understands well the differences between possession and the disorder. In his book *Uncovering the Mystery of MPD,* he suggests some guidelines for possession and for multiple personality disorder.[3]

Alter Personality	*Demon*
Most alters, even "persecutor" alters, can become strong allies. There is a definite sense of relationship with them, even if it starts out negative.	Demons are arrogant, and there is no sense of relationship with them.
Alters initially seem egodystonic but that changes to be egosyntonic over time.	Demons remain ego-alienated "outside of me."
Confusion and fear subside with appropriate therapy when only alters are present.	Confusion, fear, and lust persist despite therapy when demons are present.

Alters tend to conform to surroundings.	Demons force unwanted behavior, then blame a personality.
Alters have personalities with accompanying voices.	Demons have a negative voice which has no corresponding personality.
Irritation, discontent, and rivalry abound among alters.	Hatred and bitterness are the most common feelings among demons.
Images of alters are human in form, and remain consistent during imagery.	The imagery of demons changes between human and non-human forms, with many variations.

The final area of caution involves the false negative diagnosis of an incorrect exclusion of possession as a factor in the life of a patient with MPD. The therapist assumes that demons are only funny little characters in comic books, thereby overlooking the possibility that his multiple patient is possessed in addition to having the disorder. The therapist will never be able to successfully integrate the patient because demons cannot be integrated. That can obviously cause all kinds of untold problems in therapy and healing.

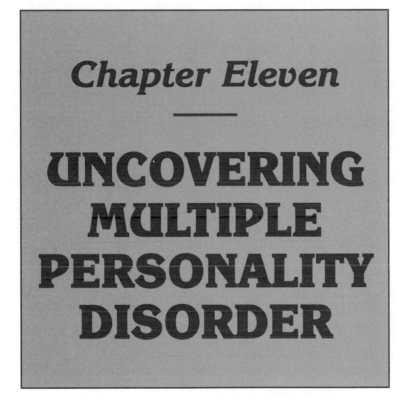

Chapter Eleven

—

UNCOVERING MULTIPLE PERSONALITY DISORDER

COLLEEN—A GIRL IN SEARCH OF HERSELF

For as long as Colleen could remember, she was always trying to please somebody in her life.

She walked a thin rope—forever working to be the person she thought everyone wanted her to be. With a practiced perfectionism, Colleen worked toward the image of the perfect woman, saying and doing everything that seemed to be correct, clever, and capable.

Her clothes were stylish fashions, designer labels that all the glamour magazines would approve of and promote. In her home, she had all the right accessories and latest kitchen gadgets. Not just any car would do; Colleen had to have an *impressive* car in her garage. The latest hit albums were in her collection. If a book had made the *New York Times* best-seller list, you knew it would be on Colleen's coffee table.

Sometimes, it was hard for Colleen to know what her own thoughts were because so many of her opinions were those of the people she admired and looked up to. After all, she was the perfect woman.

Before she came to California, Colleen had been a graduate student in English literature at a university on the East Coast. She finished with honors, all the more an accomplishment because she was holding down a full-time teaching assistant position. She was proud of her ability to be able to do so much—surely that could win the approval and acceptance of others. Call her a workaholic and Colleen would accept it as a compliment.

But the perfect woman had a terrible secret. Her facade was a burden, but it helped to block out the feeling that *sometimes her life was not really in control at all.* Colleen's life felt very much out of her control. The passage of time never seemed to be constant for her —just erratic. And she was haunted by an unknown, sinister feeling—like a dark cloud was coming down to suffocate her. She would often try to shrug it off and immerse herself in her studies. She knew the feelings were not normal. At other times, she felt the panicky, squeezed feeling and truly thought she would not make it through the week. *If I can just hold on to myself,* she would think, *if I can make it to the weekend, I can hide in my house. I won't have to deal with or talk to anybody. It will be okay then.*

But the strange, scary feelings did not end when she was by herself.

Colleen did not think of herself as suicidal, yet during the weekends she was terrified that come Monday morning someone would find her dead in her apartment. She lost track of time again and again, and she would be both bewildered and relieved to find that it was Monday morning suddenly, and that she was very much alive.

> *Her inner thoughts were voices that repeated, "If they find out what you are really like, they won't admire you. You won't be loved."*

Telling herself it was "just stress," Colleen managed to find a few therapists she could go to "as a release valve." Long-term psychotherapy was not really necessary, she reasoned; she needed something to tide her over through her "spells." She couldn't bear the thought of anyone finding out that there was something wrong, that there wasn't anything under the facade of fastidiousness. Colleen needed everyone to believe she was perfect, and she was deathly afraid someone might find out she wasn't. Her inner thoughts were voices that repeated, "If they find out what you are really like, they won't admire you. You won't be loved."

In the mid-1980s, Colleen moved to Berkeley, California, to work for a university professor. The position involved doing research on medieval English literature for an upcoming graduate-level textbook. Colleen was well suited for the job, which involved little stress and few demanding deadlines. Best of all, she found a new boyfriend. Jonathan was twelve years older, a middle-aged professor also from the English Department who served as her mentor.

Everything was perfect until the spells of dark clouds returned.

The feelings were stronger and darker. The thoughts in her head were loud, like hoofbeats. "This time they'll find you out," they said. "He'll leave you like the others when he finds out you're not for real." She tried to close her mind. "What if others could hear my thoughts?" she wondered.

Late one Friday afternoon, Colleen was packing her briefcase with journals to take home for the weekend. She considered whether to take the elevator for ease or the outside staircase because the four-story flight down had such a beautiful view over the parkway below. Nature won out. Colleen turned off the office lights, closed the door, and stepped out on the balcony outside the department offices, looking down over the railing.

"Jump," said the voice inside her head.

"I'm not suicidal," Colleen said aloud to herself. But she looked down at the expanse of hard yellow cement squares that made up the plaza forty feet below.

"Jump. Stop all the pain now. The secret won't stay."

Colleen backed inside the building and headed for the elevator.

The awful feelings were coming back. She knew they were not normal, but who could she tell? Her last therapist in Boston suggested it was a panic attack. "It's an anxiety disorder that affects many young women," the analyst said. "You're under stress. It's understandable. But it won't last more than a few weeks. Try deep breathing exercises and yoga. It will all pass within a few months."

How could Colleen tell her that the problems had been steadily growing, not subsiding? How could Colleen tell her that the feelings had been increasingly out of control and that it had been going on for years, not months? How could Colleen explain that her thoughts were also voices or that it was impossible to keep track of time? Here on the West Coast, she had no stress; she had a great job and a man who adored her. What was wrong? Why would she want to kill herself? To whom could she give her secret about the awful feelings that were going to take over and strangle her, the feeling of a tangible evil coming to get her?

And so that was how Colleen made an appointment to see me. She was afraid to let her secret out, but she was more afraid of suicide. She knew she did not want to die. She was rational enough to know that her feelings were not rational. Colleen had come across my name in a church she was visiting in southern California and called the next morning for an appointment.

PROBLEMS THAT BRING MULTIPLES INTO THERAPY

As unsensational as it may seem, that is often the state of mind of my patients with MPD when they first seek treatment. Few patients come to therapy aware that they have MPD. The following are some of the presenting problems that lead people with MPD to seek help.

Depression

The most common complaint from my patients with MPD is probably depression. It is not the kind of depression that follows a death of a loved one—such as a spouse, parent, or child. It is not the depression that follows an incident of profound loss—such as going through a divorce or getting laid off from a job. Some of my patients are overachievers, which could cause me to think that the depression is related to stress and work. But usually, I get a sense that the workaholism is part of a bigger problem that is the real catalyst of the depression.

I would describe the depression of these patients as being unsubstantive, vague, and at the same time overwhelming. They say that their lives are "out of control." They are frustrated and confused that they lose time, forget places, don't know people who recognize them, and have possessions they cannot account for.

Part of the depression is fear. Fear of finding out what is wrong. Fear of being found mentally ill. A portion of the depression is rooted in the frustration of knowing that the anxieties cannot be allayed unless they are *revealed*. Yet these anxieties cannot be revealed because the risk of being found out is too great!

The risk of being found to be mentally ill is too painful and probably all too real. They hear voices, they feel time is out of control in their lives, and they wake up in places they didn't think they had ever been. With life so confusing and unpredictable, so out of control, the depression that sets in often leads to thoughts of self-destruction and suicide.

Suicide

Most of my patients with MPD reach the black edge of despair and become suicidal. For some, it may not last long, but usually, at least one episode of feeling seriously suicidal will occur in their lives.

With one group of suicidal patients, I have determined that they have a suicidal alter personality. These patients don't seem to exhibit full-scale depression. They tell me that they have tried to commit suicide, but they are not at all sure they want to die! They describe "finding razor blades," or they "catch themselves" taking sleeping pills. In these cases, I look to uncover an alter who is suicidal; it is probably the persecutor. It sounds more like they are describing what is happening to a friend they are concerned about. Although the multiple may be bewildered or perhaps sad at times, and understandably her life-style may leave her depressed, she is not suicidal. I would place my patient Colleen in this category. Although she had some definite fears and anxieties, I could not see that she was depressed enough to end it all.

The other classification of suicidal patient with MPD is one in which the multiple is at risk. In this case, the core personality *is* suicidal and for the most part demonstrates behavior and feelings typical of a suicidal patient. She feels overwhelmed and confused. Her life is hopelessly out of control, and she feels deep psychological pain.

Anxiety

As in Colleen's case, a multiple may come into therapy because she feels troubled by generalized anxieties. The patient is at a loss to explain seemingly irrational fears or to pinpoint what precisely she feels anxious about. The memories of earlier abuse may be starting to enter consciousness, or the emotions and sensations may be tied into an event that an alter remembers and is acting out and the multiple is just starting to feel.

Time

A specific complaint from my patients involves the element of time. My patients describe it in a variety of ways: "blank spells," "lost time," "I black out," "missing time."

> *When a new patient enters my office with a complaint relating to "missing time," I consider it a tip-off that the patient may be a multiple, and I am alert to other symptoms.*

"Time makes no sense to me," said one patient with MPD. "In fact, I haven't bothered to wear a watch since my freshman year in college. It wouldn't do any good."

Obviously, the missing time element is directly related to the time in which the alters are out. Therefore, when a new patient enters my office with a complaint relating to "missing time," I consider it a tip-off that the patient may be a multiple, and I am alert to other symptoms.

Alcoholism and Drug Abuse

People with MPD may abuse alcohol, barbiturates, cocaine, and other drugs as a way of handling their fears and coping with life. Within the person who may be drinking two six-packs of beer a night is an alter personality who professes to never touch alcohol. Drugs can also be the persecutor's way of acting out self-destructive behavior. That most frequently becomes evident where drugs are used in failed suicide attempts. More often the multiple will come into therapy talking about a drug problem and then later admit it was a cover-up for other problems, such as severe depression or intense anxiety. An addiction greatly complicates the recovery process. The addiction must be treated while the multiple is manageable. If the addiction is not successfully treated, all the work with the multiple will be greatly hindered.

Sexual Dysfunction

Over half of my MPD patients exhibit sexual dysfunction in their relationships. This characteristic is not surprising, given the number of these patients who have been sexually abused during their formative years. Their feelings, emotions, and sexual orientation and expression were never properly developed and nurtured.

Just as a multiple might be an alcoholic and maintain a personality that is a teetotaler, a multiple may be a sex addict and possess one or more personalities that claim to never have sex. A multiple may state that there is no desire or ability to have sex. The confusion often leads a multiple to seek help.

RELATED DISORDERS

People with MPD are most commonly misdiagnosed for a few other psychological disorders. I list them here for two important reasons:

1. We must be able to differentiate between problems. Should you have occasion to know or help someone with MPD, it is helpful to know what the person does not have versus all that is involved with MPD.

2. When you know someone who has been in unsuccessful therapy for several years, and she talks of being treated for these related disorders (schizophrenia, borderline personality, bipolar disorder), *you can at least raise the possibility of MPD.* Initially, you will be less confused by the behavior you see, and it will eventually help the multiple when she senses you are understanding and accepting of the disorder.

One more point to consider: a person could have MPD *and* have any one of these disorders, or *an alter* could have one of these disorders. Although I have not had patients with such a combination, I have been told of a multiple with a suspected schizophrenic alter.

Schizophrenia

Schizophrenia is often mistakenly diagnosed for MPD. There are a few overt similarities:

- The patient hears voices.

- The patient exhibits bizarre or irregular behavior.

- The patient suggests that behavior is being influenced by others.

However, schizophrenia is a mental as well as a physiological illness, usually requiring a prescription drug to control the symptoms. MPD has its roots as a psychological and behavioral response. The drugs used to treat schizophrenia come under the classification of antipsychotics. For a multiple, many times not only will these drugs *not* be of any use, but these drugs may compound the problem and lead to further splitting and the creation of new alters to handle the threat of a powerful psychotropic drug.

Because of the confusion that often occurs initially between schizophrenia and MPD, I have devised a chart to distinguish some of the similar features.

Features	*Schizophrenia*	*Multiple Personality Disorder*
Voices	Are heard "outside" the head; are rambling, disjunct	Are heard "inside" the head; are lucid; hold intelligent conversations
	Are fragmentary in nature; patient finds nothing bizarre about hearing these voices	Are distinct alters; patient realizes that hearing these voices is not normal

People	Believes other people are controlling her mind or body (she hears the voices but perceives them as coming from outside herself)	Fears that other people are somehow living inside her
Causes of Irregular Behavior	Thinking processes not normal	Different alters in control of the body
Cause of Illness	Physiological imbalance in the brain	Severe child abuse or other emotional trauma early in childhood
Treatment	Prescription drugs	Long-term psychotherapy leading to integration of split personalities into a more functional person

Other Related Disorders

The presenting behavior of alter personalities—especially one such as the persecutor whose behavior is quite unlike that of the host—mimics a disorder known as borderline personality. In this disorder, the individuals have abnormally low self-esteem. They consistently act out irrationally in terms of intensity of response to a situation (losing their temper over a minor incident) or appropriateness of response (wanting to throw a huge party for a boyfriend after making up from a fight).

In the case of a multiple, the ranges of personalities in the alters would appear almost the same. For instance, one week the persecutor alter might come to the office and swear and gripe about work. The next week another alter might rave about her great job. To the unsuspecting professional, this disorder would seem to fit the behavior of a patent borderline personality so it is only natural that family members would be confused.

Another problem that might be mistakenly identified rather than MPD is manic-depression. The unnatural extreme swings in mood—from manic and expansive to depressive and hopeless—mark the personality cycles present in what is most frequently called a bipolar affective disorder. The differences between alters' personalities could easily mimic the mood swings in the bipolar disorder.

IDENTIFYING THE PROBLEM IN A FAMILY MEMBER

Some of the following symptoms are clues that might lead you to determine someone in your family has MPD. In and of themselves, these symptoms may or may not indicate MPD. However, two or more symptoms may well be a very good indication.

Childhood Amnesia

The person will be unable to give a substantial childhood history prior to the age of fifteen or sixteen. The person will say something like, "My mind is a blank, I just can't remember anything that happened to me during elementary school." Other times she will remember only two or three fragmentary snatches of life prior to the first year in high school. If she will enter therapy, she may start to remember "one more thing"—a person or an event from childhood. But basically, the memory will return (if at all) in fragments and snatches of images.

Lost Time

The element of lost or missing time is probably the key indicator for MPD. Only one other problem has lost time associated with it, and that is alcoholism. Sometimes alcoholics drink so much that nothing they do registers in the memory bank. These blackout periods find the alcoholic appearing to function normally but unable to remember anything. The progression of alcoholism is so different from MPD that it is not easy to confuse alcoholic blackouts with the lost time of a multiple. Many times, however, patients with MPD will abuse alcohol or drugs. Teasing out this combination may require professional assistance.

> *Only one other problem has lost time associated with it, and that is alcoholism.*

Referring to Self as "We"

People who refer to themselves in the first person plural are highly suspect for MPD. Theoretically, I suppose it could also be a case of schizophrenia; the person imagines he is the commander of an army or a representative of a large group of people and then is speaking for the collective. However, more often it is an alter personality who is out. In my original encounter with a multiple patient in Torrance, Lorinda referred to herself as "we." Lorinda was an alter, but she was in control more often than the core personality.

If you have a family member with MPD, it would take a lot for her to come forward and seek help. People with MPD are afraid of being "found out" that they are not normal or that they have been covering up their strange lives they do not have an explanation for—the missing time and extra clothing and strangers who know them by different names.

The wonderful thing about this disorder is that once a multiple is in counseling with a competent therapist, there is hope for a full recovery of symptoms and a cohesive, integrated life. Multiple personality disorder is very treatable.

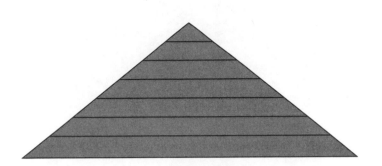

Section 3

SPIRITUAL-
ITY

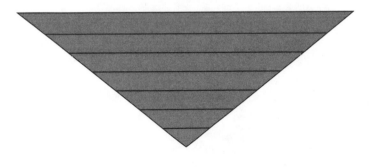

Chapter Twelve

—

PATRICIA REMEMBERS

Two years prior to her seeing me, as a thirty-three-year-old wife and mother, Patricia remembered carrying the groceries through the back door of her modest home in the San Gabriel Valley. She was anxious to get dinner started so that it could be ready and waiting for her husband, Richard, when he came home from work at six o'clock. She placed two bags of groceries on the counter and went back to retrieve her little boy who had fallen asleep in his car seat. After settling Davey in the playpen and surrounding him with his favorite playthings, she went into the kitchen to prepare dinner.

Pat is a talented, brilliant woman. She graduated second in her class at Radcliffe and went on to receive her master's degree in physics. Pat had married her childhood sweetheart from Maryland ten years earlier, and three years ago they moved to California where he was a programmer for an insurance corporation. Pat considered herself blessed to have such a good husband, healthy child, and pleasant home.

As she proceeded with her dinner preparations, she

> *Patricia tried desperately to blink away the vision, but it stayed before her, playing out like a videotape for almost twenty seconds.*

was jolted by a long-buried memory of carnage in which she took part. Patricia tried desperately to blink away the vision, but it stayed before her, playing out like a videotape for almost twenty seconds. Pat was both mortified and mystified.

The strange episode intensified her feelings of hopelessness and helplessness that had been building over the years. It was not anything that she could exactly put her finger on, but Patricia had always struggled with depression. Even with her excellent education, she was having difficulty holding down a full-time job due to the generalized anxieties.

Six weeks later, a different version of the same thing happened. And two weeks after that, Pat had another vision of violent events she knew nothing about. Pat was stumped and bewildered. She had already decided she needed to see a counselor about her depression and anxieties, but the visions prompted her to move to make an appointment. Patricia confessed to using drugs and alcohol during her teens and early twenties, and she wondered if the visions were latent hallucinations stemming from her substance abuse.

> *If an event is traumatic enough, it is often repressed or blocked out from the memory.*

After several visits, the counselor explained to her that the visions were probably flashbacks of events that had taken place in her life. He explained further that if an event is traumatic enough, it is often repressed or blocked out from the memory. It then may be brought to the conscious mind through a series of flashbacks—as though the mind were presenting a series of snapshots of the event.

EVIDENCE DISCLOSED

The flashbacks increased, and Patricia became more and more distressed. She was unable to sleep at night. She was hospitalized for stabilization. As scenes from her childhood returned through the flashbacks, other difficult memories began to surface as well. The counselor took a family history and was shocked to find that four of Pat's cousins, two nieces, one nephew, and one brother had committed suicide. There was definite evidence for early childhood trauma.

As more and more evidence was uncovered, the truth eventually was revealed. Patricia's entire extended family was involved in an underground satanic cult that met in the hills in a deserted barn.

At the age of three, Patricia began her involuntary initiation into the cult. The cult members would nail her and several snakes into a coffin. Even at her young age, Patricia learned that if she held perfectly still, the snakes would curl up and nest beside her rather than slither their cold, hard bodies across her arms and legs every time she wiggled.

At four years old, she was regularly stripped naked and tied down on an altar, where the cult men and women sexually abused her.

At five years of age, she was sexually stimulated by the cult witches, other times hung upside down with her feet and arms tied together, and other times forced to sacrifice animals in the rituals.

By her seventh birthday, Patricia had also watched the human sacrifices. Later the remains were hung in a small room under the barn where the cult met, and Patricia would be tied up next to them. Other times for discipline she would be chained up in the barn overnight with nowhere to go to the bathroom.

As a punishment for a minor infraction when she was ten years old, Patricia was marched out to the woodshed and had her hand hammered into a shelf. She later wiggled free, but to this day she bears a deep scar in the palm and on the back of her hand.

By the time she was eleven, Pat and some of the other

selected girls in the cult were trained to be high priestesses. Their duties and first chores were to help with the festivities and to make preparations for the night rituals.

Two weeks after Patricia's thirteenth birthday, she was hospitalized for a short while in a psychiatric hospital. While she was a patient there, another patient raped her, and she became pregnant. At seven months gestation, her uncles and parents tied her down onto a bed and then abused her until she aborted the stillborn fetus.

When Patricia was seventeen, she ran away from home with several other friends, two of whom had been abused in the rituals. Unfortunately, the girls were discovered by two policemen who also happened to be members of the cult. After their return home, Patricia and her friends were punished for their disobedience. "Don't ever think of leaving or trying to get away from where you know you belong," they were warned. "The only way you'll be out of here is through your own death."

PAT'S BELIEF SYSTEM

This record of Patricia's life (and I am omitting much) was pieced together over several years of therapy. Pat was hospitalized twice more for stabilization, and then last year she was hospitalized for suicidal tendencies as more of her horror was revealed.

At that point, I came to see Patricia for therapy. She couldn't sleep, and she was frightened by her flashbacks.

It was probably more difficult for Pat to believe that

those things had happened to her than it was for me. I had worked with other multiples and with patients who had been through similar ritual abuse. I was not at all surprised that she could not remember what had taken place in her life—a blank is commonplace.

Because I was so accepting of what she said and what she thought she was remembering, Patricia was able to build trust with me. In particular, I had gained the trust of one alter—the rescuer—who filled me in on much valuable information. The rescuer knew that Patricia was terrified that the cult would find her and come and kill her or, worse yet, would take her son and force her to watch him being sacrificed. That was apparently something she had seen happen to at least one set of parents in a ritual.

Pat had become a churchgoing Christian who believed in God. Her strong belief was intriguing to me because throughout her life, she had been indoctrinated to believe that Jesus was a liar and that all Christians were hateful hypocrites. Her church was important to her, and those who knew of her background were extremely supportive and tried to provide her with safety —both spiritually and physically. But many did not believe her story was true. I think one reason she trusted me as her therapist was that I'm a Christian. She knew I had already dealt with other patients who had been involved with cults, and therefore, would be more likely to believe the things she remembered.

Although her belief system was centered on Christianity, Patricia was terribly fearful of her relatives and anyone else from the cult. After the "suicides" of her cousins, she knew what could happen if she left the cult. Those of us in mental health have an extra challenge

> *After the "suicides" of her cousins, she knew what could happen if she left the cult.*

when treating people with MPD who have been in ritual abuse. We are patching wounds, healing memories, deprogramming the brainwashing, and struggling to help deeply wounded people recover.

Chapter Thirteen

SATANIC RITUAL ABUSE

Can you imagine that across the nation, hundreds of children are being systematically tortured, terrorized, and brainwashed? Would you believe that the perpetrators are people involved in underground satanic cults? Is it conceivable that this activity continues under a cloak of secrecy and without most of the U.S. population knowing of its existence? The abuse I will be addressing in this chapter is so widespread and occurs with such regularity *that it has been identified by both law enforcement and mental health professionals.* It is called satanic ritual abuse, referred to as SRA or ritual abuse. It is a major factor in the increase of MPD in North America.

The concept of satanic ritual abuse is even more difficult for people to believe and accept than the concept of MPD. People may be loath to make definitive statements about anything that smacks of religion, but they will especially shy away from anything that touches on "evil" themes. I find that this reticence stems not so much from a fear of evil or powers of darkness but from the notion that the whole subject of evil seems "hokey" and too silly to be taken seriously for discussion. However, you do not have to believe in either God or Satan to understand that any behavior that harms, hurts, or terrorizes children is unjustified. At some level within your moral system, you must be able to view this purposeful, systematized abuse as inherently evil.

We know that some people have decided to worship the devil as an act of religious freedom. Some of these practices deliver more into the creation of evil than the free practice of religion. When their religious rituals involve harming children physically, psychologically, or emotionally, we must be willing to speak out and do everything to stop this abuse. I do not wish to make an exposé of satanic ritual abuse here because many other books and reports cover the subject more thoroughly and extensively than I can. (See "Resources.") However, I do wish to address the issue because of its predominance in MPD.

Before we proceed, we need to turn to Dr. Lawrence Pazder, a pioneer in the field of ritual abuse in North America, who gave this definition of *ritual abuse:* "Repeated physical, emotional, mental and spiritual assaults combined with a systematic use of symbols, ceremonies and machinations designed and orchestrated to attain malevolent effects."

DIFFERENTIATING PHYSICAL, SEXUAL, AND RITUAL ABUSE

You may ask, "Why differentiate physical and sexual child abuse from ritual abuse? As horrible as it may sound, isn't it ultimately all the same for the child? After enduring terror and pain and psychological torture, does it really matter for a person with MPD and her therapists that the nature of the abuse originated from a cult ritual rather than her home?"

The answer is yes—there is a significant difference. If I have a patient who is a multiple because of satanic ritual abuse, this factor will affect not only our therapeutic relationship but also the healing process and the course of the therapy.

Here are some of the ways I assess the major differences between traditional abuse and ritual abuse:

Traditional Abuse	*Ritual Abuse*
There is one perpetrator.	There are many perpetrators.
The perpetrator is known to the child, i.e., it is a parent or family member or primary caregiver.	Most of the perpetrators are not family members; they may or may not be known by the child. Family members can also be perpetrators.
There is one victim, i.e., the child.	There are often several victims or several children abused at the same time. Adults are also abused.
The abuse is usually spontaneous in nature.	The abuse has been well thought out and planned beforehand.
Alters are created inadvertently by the child (without the knowledge of the perpetrator) to protect the child from the pain and memory of the abuse.	Alters are intentionally created by the cult to serve the cult and to cause harm to the child if she should ever reveal the secret or attempt to tell or leave the cult as an adult.
The abuse seems to be usually without purpose except in and of itself or for control.	The abuse is meaningful to the cult and is a necessary part of the rituals.

The abuse is centered on or about the child's physical being.	The abuse involves external tools and events, i.e., the torture and mutilation of animals and others.
The abuse is centered on the physical and often includes emotional or psychological terror.	The abuse is strategically designed to produce pain as well as psychological and emotional terror; threats and intimidation are commonplace.
Spirituality is not an overriding factor.	The spirituality of the cult is the chief factor or component of the abuse.
The perpetrator enforces physical control over the life and well-being of the child.	The cult attempts to gain complete mind control.
There is rigid spiritual upbringing (if any).	Satan is the center of the universe.
Cognitive belief resulting is "God is a vengeful God who will punish me for my naughtiness."	Cognitive belief resulting is "God wants to destroy me because I am evil and beyond all hope. God is not as strong as Satan."
"I do not feel in control of my life."	"Satan controls my life."

LEVELS AND ORGANIZATION OF DEVIL WORSHIP

To comprehend what SRA is all about, we need to have a basic understanding of the structure and nature of devil worship in America. It is by no means a new phenomenon in this country, although it is rarely discussed. Certainly, it has not been recognized by the public on the same level as other cults, such as that at

Jonestown or the followers of Reverend Moon (the Moonies).

The Orthodox Church of Satan

Researchers in the field of cults and religion have identified three levels of Satan worship in this country. On the first level is the organized, legally recognized Church of Satan. In the mid-1960s, Anton La Vey started his Church of Satan in San Francisco. The people who attend this church openly worship the devil and use the Satanic Bible, also created by La Vey as their scripture. Regular services are held, which essentially parody and mock traditional Christian rituals with inverted crosses, scriptures, and symbols. The Church of Satan holds a Black Mass, which is a travesty of the Mass of the Roman Catholic church and its Communion rite.

> *Researchers in the field of cults and religion have identified three levels of Satan worship in this country.*

The Church of Satan exists under the full protection of the United States Constitution. Though members of the Church of Satan firmly reject any Christian beliefs and standards, they do not practice or condone any illegal activities, including animal sacrifices and drug use. The Church of Satan is considered to be orthodox and aboveboard. The members see their church as a human potential movement to develop whatever means and capabilities necessary for the members to excel as individuals.

In the Nine Satanic Statements of the Church of Satan (loosely, their code of ethics), Satan is expressed to be representing

- indulgence over abstinence.

- vital existence over spiritual pipe dreams.

- vengeance over "turn the other cheek."

- man as an animal rather than a divine or an intellectual creation.

- undefiled wisdom instead of hypocritical self-deceit.

- all of sin—as it leads to physical, mental, or emotional gratification.[1]

Self-Styled Satanists

The second level has the smallest membership of devil worshipers. These people may be subdivided into two groups and referred to as the self-styled satanists and the experimental satanists. These individuals adopt many satanic symbols and rites and paraphernalia for their own use and rituals.

Most of the people involved at this experimental level are high-school boys who fantasize about the power, have a thrill-seeking curiosity about dabbling with demons, and enjoy the vicarious association with danger and morbidity. For the most part, they are only experimenting and acting out fantasy games with satanic themes. However, there is always a possibility they will progress to the next group.

The other individuals involved as self-styled satanists are mentally disturbed and/or under the influence of drugs and alcohol. They commit acts of murder, vandalism, mutilation, theft, and rape as part of their self-imposed allegiance to the devil. They created their belief system and practice it on their own. They may use their belief system to justify their criminal behavior, or the behavior may stem from their mentally disturbed condition, which is wrapped around their selective self-imposed rituals. A number of serial killers, such as Richard Ramirez, the "Night Stalker," are devil worshipers on this level.

Underground Satanic Cults

The third level of devil worship in America may not be the largest, but it is probably the most dangerous. It is the familial or generational underground cult worship of Satan. This group demands secrecy and loyalty from its membership. Members must swear their allegiance to Satan and the cult leaders, and they are threatened with harm if they leave the cult and with death if they reveal the secret.

These satanic cults involve numerous families or family clans and operate secretly, most often in private homes, forests, or deserted barns or other isolated buildings. A typical cult may have two hundred to four hundred members; they break up into smaller clans of thirty

> *Members must swear their allegiance to Satan and the cult leaders, and they are threatened with harm if they leave the cult and with death if they reveal the secret.*

to fifty people. The rituals are filled with drug-induced orgiastic episodes in which rape, torture, mutilation, animal sacrifice, human sacrifice, and cannibalism are regularly featured. To support these activities, the members may traffic in drugs and steal. This level of satanists operates completely outside the law and, therefore, is not protected constitutionally, even though it may be considered a religion in some sense of the word.

This cult is often multigenerational and intergenerational in that entire families participate—cousins, aunts, grandparents, and so on. One is usually "born" into this cult from within the family, although the total cult membership will also include unrelated people from the community along with their families.

These cults are largely made up of professional people in well-respected careers—from bankers, nurses, doctors, and judges to police officers, schoolteachers, stockbrokers, elected officials, and preachers. The horrifying part about this membership is that the cult secret can be preserved when its members are so highly placed in society—positions that would enable them to prevent exposure and to hide or destroy evidence.

It is this third level of satanic cult with which we are involved when we discuss satanic ritual abuse.

SATANIC RITUAL ABUSE

I have given the overview above because when you understand that a satanic cult hates God and is opposed to everything that would be considered near and dear to God, you can begin to see why these cults target children. If the Scriptures describe children as being special and loved by God, what better way to seek revenge on God than by either destroying the ones He loves or training them to serve God's chief adversary?

If what I am about to describe seems too unbelievable, let me assure you it is believable when you are dealing with it on a weekly or sometimes daily basis, and it is happening.

Psychiatrists are trained to deal with symptoms. When patients come to them with physical and emotional ills, psychiatrists will work to discern the cause and to relieve the pain. When patients tell stories about torture in satanic rituals, most mental health professionals tend to distance themselves. But over the last fifteen years, psychiatrists have started to compare notes. Maybe a psychologist is referring a patient and says, "This girl relates stories about killing her baby and drinking blood for a weird ritual." The doctor might say, "That's funny. Another therapist is telling me she has a patient saying the exact same thing." They go to a conference and discuss the patients only to discover that two associates from the East Coast and a psychologist from the South have patients with the same story themes. They have to start thinking that is more than a coincidence. The point is, these rituals are being described by people from every area throughout the United States and Canada, and by people who are unrelated and unconnected to each other. The themes of these macabre tales have been repeated so often, and the methods of abuse sufficiently standardized, that this activity has now been identified and labeled by the mental health community and the law enforcement community as SRA—Satanic Ritual Abuse.

Some people have difficulty comprehending what actually happens in satanic ritual abuse because it touches on religion and people are reticent to deal with religion. If people are uncomfortable discussing a personal God, they are even more uncomfortable admitting to the existence of the devil, evil spirits, and demons. Once the term *satanic* is referenced, people have a hard time accepting the diagnosis. For that reason, some people in mental health refer to all of this as *ritual abuse.* This term then includes any other abusive religious rite, and it allows people to look at what is happening and to call it as they see it. I call it evil because someone does not have to be a religious or churchgoing person to understand what evil is or how it affects children when it involves pain, degradation, torture, rape, and terror.

ELEMENTS OF SRA

Although no two cults hold absolutely identical rituals and ceremonies, many features seem to be regular components and are reported by children as young as three to adult women in their thirties and forties who start remembering the events initially through flashbacks.

The following are the most frequently cited rituals:

- *Threats/intimidations.* Young children are threatened with death if they should ever tell the secret; if their parents are not members of the cult (the children are brought in by other relatives or by preschool or day-care workers), the children are told their parents will be killed.

- *Stripping.* All victims, regardless of age, are stripped and made to feel vulnerable and unprotected both physically and psychologically. Most of the young children describe being photographed in the nude. The victims are inspected and sexually molested by both men and women in the cult.

- *Penetration.* Besides being raped, children are penetrated with all kinds of ritual elements, crucifixes, knives, candles, snakes, and so on. Quite often, children will describe that "they put sticks inside me and the other children."

- *Drugs.* Both children and adults are given drugs; children usually describe being given a "punch to drink that made me feel sleepy [or funny or sick]."

- *Mutilation of animals.* Small animals, usually cats, rabbits, or dogs, are mutilated before the young children who are threatened with the same fate if they should tell anyone.

- *Burial.* A child between the ages of three and six is put inside a coffin, and then spiders, snakes, and/or rodents are added to terrorize the child. The child is lowered into a hole. Later a cult official will rescue the child, further confusing her; she now is impressed to owe her life to her captor.

- *Breeders.* Teenage girls are impregnated by the men in the cult. Later when she is at full term, the girl will be given a drug to induce labor at the ceremony. When the baby is born, it is sacrificed on the spot during the ritual. Often the girl is forced to kill it herself. Almost all mutilations and killings are done with a ceremonial knife.

- *Marriage ceremony.* The victim is stripped and "married" to a high priest or consecrated to Satan. The child is then said to "belong" to Satan.[2]

Part and parcel of almost every cult ritual are torture, mutilation (carving initials into the victims), and molestation.

I understand that if this is the first time you have been confronted with this information, it is almost too much to believe. The first time I encountered satanic ritual abuse in one of my patients, it was very difficult for me to accept or comprehend. However, as repeated stories were related by new patients, I had to consider it all in a new light. One thing I am struck by is that the stories are related with such clarity and detail. The information, however fantastic, always smacks of the truth, and any information that can be verified always checks out.

I remember talking to one patient, Jennifer, who had been involved in the cult since she was born. Jennifer described in great detail how the cult would sacrifice young children. It had happened apparently more than once. I knew how baby sacrifices were covered up—the cult induced labor in the mother and killed the baby on the spot so that there was no record of the birth and no record of the death. But the children she described were between four and ten years old. I asked her where the children came from. Jennifer explained they were part of the one to two hundred "missing children" reported each year. (More than that are reported missing, but most are abducted by divorced parents; law enforcement figures are that less than two hundred annually are abducted by strangers.) I asked Jennifer how it was possible that adults were snatching children and were never noticed or caught.

Being a mother myself, I'll never forget her response. She said, "Oh, the adults don't get these children. That is the job of the kids in the cult. They entice other children to follow them back to a house or car for candy or toys. The cult knows that people will never notice children talking to other children. And children are never or rarely afraid of other children." An older child of twelve or thirteen will be trained to abduct a toddler or child and later participate in the sacrifice of his or her abductee.

DIFFICULTIES IN TREATING
SRA MULTIPLES

With these facts in mind, we can now look at the impact of this abuse on people with multiple personalities.

The first is the issue of trust. A therapist must work carefully to build and gain the trust of any multiple patient. However, multiples who have undergone satanic ritual abuse are extremely reluctant to trust anyone. If they have grown up in the cult, they know that cult members include people from every level of the community. They have been betrayed not only by their families but by the very people who traditionally are considered to be in positions of protection and healing—police officers, doctors, and church members.

Because the stories sound so absolutely unbelievable, therapists are inclined not to believe them. That is part of the entrapment of the cult. The victims have nowhere to go when they are younger because the cult is all around them; when they are older, they have nowhere to go because who is going to believe their stories? How could any rational professional consider that these events could really happen? (That is why it is an incredible blessing for SRA victims to find professionals who have dealt with other ritual abuse victims; not only are they believed, but the therapists can substantiate and validate their claims from what they know from prior patients.) And people with MPD may have the very real fear that the *therapists* could be associated with the cult and cause them harm.

Apparently, these cults have discovered that very bright and creative children may dissociate from the trauma and develop MPD. The cults cultivate alters for use in the rituals and train them to respond to given signals. A cult is able to give a key word or secret symbol to a multiple, which will engage the cult alter to switch out, take control of the body, and engage in cult rituals or command an "unwilling" multiple to return to the cult.

One very complicated multiple patient was a victim of satanic ritual abuse. The complication was that she still had two alters who were going to the cult! It is

> *A cult is able to give a key word or secret symbol to a multiple, which will engage the cult alter to switch out, take control of the body, and engage in cult rituals or command an "unwilling" multiple to return to the cult.*

practically impossible to treat a multiple and bring her to health and healing when she is still involved with the source of her pain and dissociation. I would be trying to bring out the bad memories and all that she had been through, and the following week the alters would go back to the cult where they would be tortured and raped.

Certain times of the year are significant for cults. All of the solstices, each full moon, Friday the Thirteenth, and so on figure prominently in cult rituals. But one of the most important is Halloween. I was extremely worried about one multiple patient who was hospitalized during a significant period of satanic activity. I recommended hospitalization because she had deteriorated and I wanted to protect her from the cult. I had to instruct the hospital staff that she was absolutely not to have any visitors or phone calls, nor could any packages be brought in. It would take just a telephone call, and a secret word could trigger a cult alter to come out and return to the cult. Or cult members could send a package containing an innocuous-looking item—stone, seashell, candle, or mirror with a symbol painted on the back—which would trigger a response from the appropriate alter.

One last problem is that these cult alters are also trained to self-destruct if the multiple should reveal the secret and talk about the cult and its activities. Basically, the alter will try to kill the multiple—jumping, overdosing, or cutting her wrists. While multiples in general may be suicidal, there is a different element with cult multiples who have been preprogrammed for self-destruction. I work to keep the multiple in these situations as safe and protected as possible while trying to gain the trust of the stronger alters. In these cases, I try to let the protector or rescuer alter know to be on guard for seriously suicidal behavior from cult alters. Sometimes, I may not have met the cult alters, but if I learn that the multiple has been involved heavily in a cult, I definitely suspect the others are around.

Dr. Lawrence Pazder coined the phrase "ritualized abuse" and made these comments at the annual meeting of the American Psychiatric Association in New Orleans in 1980:

> It's hard for people to believe there is a secret underworld where cults thrive as people are destroyed. When you look at the devastation and fragmentation of multiples, you become convinced that nothing ordinary

> *Satanic ritual abuse is a real phenomenon. It is known and documented by clinicians, politicians, and law enforcement officials.*

could have produced these kinds of problems and reactions. There is horror and hopelessness for the MPD but with time and hard work, there is a way out.[3]

Satanic ritual abuse is a real phenomenon. It is known and documented by clinicians, politicians, and law enforcement officials. I believe those of us who know this to be true have a professional responsibility. That responsibility varies for each of us. For me, acknowledgment and validation of SRA are part of the educational process for which I feel responsible as a doctor. For others, exposure of cults is an issue. Police departments are aware of their existence. Prosecutions, however, are hampered by the secrecy of the cults and coconspirators. Generally, I do not feel my life is in direct danger from the cults as long as I keep my distance from their turf. At times patients have expressed a fear for my safety due to the awareness of cult members that I have advised and encouraged the patients to withdraw from the cult. So far, nothing dangerous has happened to me, although my patients have at times been tormented with finding skinned cats or dead rabbits on their doorsteps. While some cult members have come to the hospital to talk to the multiple, their more usual pattern is to keep a very low profile with me and other authority figures. They don't want to be found out, and remaining unknown to me maintains their secrecy and existence. I do believe that should I or any therapist take on a primary responsibility for revealing the cult, there could be direct danger. All clinicians should carefully consider this potential dilemma.

Chapter Fourteen

———

SUCCESSFUL THERAPY

HELEN'S HAPPY ENDING

Helen doesn't look like someone who has been hospitalized seventeen times in the past twenty years. Her calm face and engaging smile belie any troubles or pain that could have been in her past. But she grew up in a home where her grandfather locked her up in a closet from the time she was old enough to stand. She often hid from her grandfather when he came home after drinking, so he wouldn't find her, strip her, and whip her with his belt. Her grandfather frequently raped her —and even brought in one of his friends to molest her as well.

Helen is a professional career woman, a Realtor in Ventura County, California. With a trim, lithe figure, strawberry blond hair, and a smooth complexion, Helen easily looks ten years younger than her thirty-nine years. Her straightforward, up-front manner is appreciated by her clientele and valued by her company. She is a woman who has her act together, people say.

But things were not always this way. Helen had multiple personality disorder and within her lived thirteen separate and distinct personalities.

Luckily for Helen, she was finally able to find a competent, caring therapist who recognized her disorder. I was familiar with her story since she was in counseling with an associate, and I had seen her briefly to prescribe medication.

Helen was a classic textbook case of the course of treatment that takes place in the life of someone with MPD. She had been in and out of psychiatric wards and the offices of psychologists and psychiatrists since she was twenty. She had been diagnosed at various times as having schizophrenia, borderline personality, and chronic depression. Finally, after fourteen years in the mental health system, she happened upon a therapist who had worked with several multiple patients. He studied her medical history and interviewed and observed her over several sessions. In less than three weeks, he determined that Helen had MPD.

Over the course of three and a half years of intense therapy, Helen joined forces with her alters—Tough Lady, Fred, Little Freddie, Mrs. Snyder, Inner Mind, Angry One, Erena, Conifer, Little Helen, Patrick, Pauline, Space Cadet, and Maybelline. A motley crew as individuals yesterday, they lend a rich dimension to her life in terms of skills, emotions, and knowledge now that they are integrated and fused with Helen's personality. She had one relapse—six months after fusion when her sister died in a terrible car accident—but after another year of therapy, Helen's integration held, and she was pronounced successfully fused.

> *Over the course of three and a half years of intense therapy, Helen joined forces with her alters—Tough Lady, Fred, Little Freddie, Mrs. Snyder, Inner Mind, Angry One, Erena, Conifer, Little Helen, Patrick, Pauline, Space Cadet, and Maybelline.*

THE PATIENT'S THOUGHTS

How does Helen feel today? I asked her to give me her thoughts about being a "whole" person now that she has been integrated for three years.

She makes no bones about the difficulty of treatment itself: "Sometimes I felt like I could never be normal. It was hard to imagine that things were ever going to get better. It's painful to go through therapy, and it was painful to remember and relive all the things that happened to me. It was hard to face those things emotionally because the people who did those things were the people who were supposed to love me and protect me. It made me angry, too—which was the first good sign that therapy was getting through to me. I never knew how to feel angry before that.

"Initially, the only way I could keep going back [to therapy] was that Mark [the therapist] allowed me to hope. He kept on encouraging me and making me believe that things could be normal, whatever that was. He allowed me to believe that the day would actually come when I could feel like I would fit in and I could feel like I belonged the way other people do. But at the same time it was hard, painful work. It's not a short, snap job by any means. Life is either upside down or up and down; a real roller coaster.

"After all is said and done, I would never trade where I am today for where I was before therapy. The shadows are gone in my life. The most amazing thing I noticed right off the bat is that there is so much more *time* during the day. It feels like a gift. There are no surprises. Everything is where I left it. I know all the people in my life now. I am in control of my life, my time, and my possessions.

"I was afraid to be integrated, and I know Tough Lady and Pauline [two very strong alters] were really very worried about fusion. But it is really true what Mark said, that none of the personalities would be lost because they were all truly part of me to begin with. Not separate people, but separate parts of my own personality and who I was and am now. They are all a part of me now. But even I am not the same as I was before integration. I was only a part before. Now I have the strength of everybody.

"We all feared the idea of integration and fusion. We

were, most of us, afraid to give up ourselves to become Somebody Else—especially when we didn't know who that Somebody Else would be or what it would feel like. Now I know. It feels freeing—there are no dark edges or boundaries or shadows. It feels safe.

"At first it felt like we were walking together—all of the alters and I were clumped together like a tight troop. I could sense the different emotions of all of the alters filtering through me constantly. At the same time I was all of the alters simultaneously. We were there once! It is just too hard to explain now. I would look in a store window and see a fashionable dress and admire it, and then stop and think to myself, *That's Erena— she's the part of me that is liking that dress!*

"Or another time at my bank, just a few months after fusion, this new teller was being an absolute idiot. She was giving me—a regular, long-term, faithful customer —a hard time about a mistake the bank was actually responsible for on my account. I know that in the past, before integration, I would have been a mouse and let her screw up my account and treat me that way. But now I could feel Angry One assert herself to straighten things out. It was Angry One and yet it was me—but it was the skills I had always delegated to Angry One's personality. But this time her response was reasonable and not out of control; it felt good to stay with it and not disappear.

"People have no idea that I had multiple personality disorder, and I don't tell most of them. Some of my close coworkers and other close friends I have told, but I don't expect them to really understand. I'm still not so sure all of them really understand what a multiple is. Most of them have read *Sybil,* so that gives them an idea, but they are usually reacting to the physical abuse in the story. I know they could never understand the emotional pain, the confusion, and the overwhelming loneliness.

"My life seems so much more simple now in some ways, more complex in other ways—it's frightening at first to realize it is me making all the decisions now and taking responsibility for it, too! I still see a therapist about once a month or so—a different one from Mark—but this is just for traditional problems. It's funny, but I so enjoy having regular problems like everybody else! I am dealing with general insecurities, and learning about healthy relationships. I have had a steady boyfriend for five months now, who has been quite supportive and understanding. His best friend in junior and senior high came from an alcoholic and physically abusive home, so there are some elements of my life that he can tap into and comprehend.

"I think the thing that I would want to convey to people is that multiples are not monsters or freak show items. We have been through horrendous pain—and not just physical. All of it is real, and all of us [meaning the alters, too] are bright personalities. . . . We don't ask you for your pity, just your understanding.

"To other multiples, I would want to convey to you that YES—YOU CAN DO IT. Hang in there—with a good therapist, with your supportive friends, and with whatever counseling you can get because it is worth it. A full, integrated life is the most peaceful existence. You will have the gift of sleep. You will have the gift of time. I know it is difficult now because it has been difficult for everyone who has started in the process of healing. Remember that many before you have made it through to

> *"Multiples are not monsters or freak show items. . . . We don't ask you for your pity, just your understanding."*

the other side. *We* made it and you can do it, too. Don't be afraid of integration and fusion—everything feels fine. You will not lose anything. In every possible way I want to tell other multiples to stay with your dream because the nightmare *will* end."

THE THERAPIST'S THOUGHTS

Without a doubt, the most rewarding aspect of my profession is seeing the mending of broken lives. I find it particularly heartening that people can overcome traumatic beginnings, emotional pain, and mental disorders and go forward to experience life at its fullest.

My favorite word for my patients is *hope.* I love to let my patients know when and where there are possibilities for health and wholeness—even though none of us have a "happily ever after." Therapy can be a mechanism for understanding limitations and opportunities, recognizing what *are* realistic dreams and how to set about achieving them. To know what is *possible* is to know about hope. Or to paraphrase Helen's words slightly, "to go forward with your dreams knowing that your nightmare will be ending."

Patients with MPD have good reason to hope because their disorder is treatable. Naturally, they may not believe that at first. They have undergone more abuse as children than most prisoners of war have seen as adults. They grew up being told they were bad. They were locked up in psychiatric wards because they were told they were mentally ill. They may have been told they were possessed. They were made to feel physically, emotionally, and spiritually defective.

Patients with MPD are *not* defective.[1] Quite the opposite. They are gifted, and this gift has allowed them to survive. Dr. Jim Friesen draws this analogy between MPD and a computer. This computer is an excellent piece of hardware, but it has a virus. However, the software with the virus does not affect new files that are created because they are not connected so they work just fine! Computers that do not have this ability to dissociate and start over cannot fight the effects of the virus and will not be able to run at all.

VARIABLES FOR SUCCESSFUL THERAPY

For people with MPD, the prognosis is very positive that they will be able to live safe, sane, and satisfying lives. They will be able to uncover the memories and survive. They will be able to pool the collective talents of their alters and use these abilities in a healthy way. They will be able to have time operate for them in much the same way it works in the rest of the world—for twenty-four hours a day, seven days a week. But a few variables can affect the successful outcome of therapy.

Motivated Patients

What kind of patient will be successful in therapy? Obviously, a motivated patient is a crucial component in this picture because the patient will go through many traumatic changes and episodes within the course of treatment. At first, the patient will not even know that she has MPD. But if she recognizes that things are not right in her life and if she feels that knowing what is wrong is preferable to living with an unknown, she is in a good position to start therapy.

This motivation and determination to get at the truth will ultimately help the patient with MPD to overcome her disorder and to regain her life.

Stable Environment

Another factor for these patients is that they should be in a stable environment. That is, if they are in the process of getting a divorce, overcoming a drug addiction, changing careers, or having major health problems, they may be overwhelmed by trying to work on therapy at the same time. Not only will attention be split and energies be absorbed with these more immediate and pressing situations, but these life catastrophes may cause more splitting and dissociation. Before embarking on the process of integration and fusion, stability in life and resolution of major stressors should be achieved in therapy.

If the patient has been a victim of ritual abuse, he

needs to be out of contact with the cult and with any of its members. It is just about impossible to work on healing with any patient if he is still living or dealing regularly with an abusive situation. Even if the patient claims he is not attending the cult rites, if he is still in communication with any of its members, he will probably be dragged back in before too long. Or if these members find out the patient is in therapy, they will fear he might expose the cult, and the cultists may try to acccss the cult alters to commit suicide or command the multiple to return to the cult.

A support system is part of a stable environment. It is impossible to predict what will come out once the therapy begins, but there are likely to be some rough times ahead. Support of friends and family will be critical. It is essential for the patient to have someone to talk to and be with before he or she embarks on the discovery and uncovering process of fusion.

Skilled Clinician

The other side of the coin in successful therapy is finding a good therapist. The first step would be to find a therapist who could recognize MPD, and the second step would be to find a therapist who is familiar with the treatment of these patients. Not every therapist who can diagnose MPD will treat these patients—but hopefully can make a referral to someone who does.

The more often that a therapist has dealt with multiples, the more likely that the therapist has gained confidence and competence in dealing with MPD. However, the patient may be the first in a particular geographic area with MPD, and therefore, the therapist is dealing with MPD for the first time. A motivated therapist who is committed to the patient's recovery and who is resourceful enough to tap into the research and experience of others in the field will be able to successfully care for the patient.

Length of Treatment

The length of time for the treatment of MPD varies from patient to patient. A tremendous amount of work is to be done between the therapist and the patient. The multiple has spent a lifetime using dissociation as a response, so it will hardly be an overnight process to undo this learned response. The personalities of the alters will also affect treatment. A persecutor alter that is a particularly strong and antisocial personality can impede the time in therapy.

The experience and the innate psychological skills of the therapist can affect the length of treatment. The time and scheduling of the patient have to be considered; a patient with a weekly one-and-a-half-hour appointment will progress more slowly than a patient who has two or three sessions a week with the therapist. An inpatient setting will often allow the patient to move along more quickly in psychotherapy than outpatient treatment.

Studies done on MPD treatment indicate that the majority of multiples can be integrated within two to three years after a correct diagnosis has been made.[2] (Most multiples have been in treatment for various psychiatric ills for an average of six and a half years before being diagnosed with MPD.) The length of time involved is usually a reflection of the number of alters of the multiple. A patient with seven alters will be more rapidly integrated than a patient with thirty personalities.

I would caution, however, that the two to three years of therapy are only a guideline, not an absolute guaran-

> *The majority of multiples can be integrated within two to three years after a correct diagnosis has been made.*

tee. Each patient with MPD is absolutely unique. Her background, her level of abuse, the number of personalities in her alter system, the age that she experienced abuses, the level of safety and security in her present life, and other predisposing factors will affect the course and time of treatment.

Patients with more than one hundred alters, known as supermultiples, have to be very carefully handled in integration because so many of these alter personalities are personality fragments. The alters were created for a one-time purpose and are exactly what their name implies—fragments of personalities. Because they are so fleeting, they may be difficult for the therapist to find, yet all must be uncovered so that the multiple can achieve successful integration.

In general, motivated patients who have been diagnosed with multiple personality disorder should antici-pate being in therapy from two and a half to four years minimally, depending on the frequency of counseling sessions. Regardless of the time factor, patients should be reminded that they have spent at least twenty years of their lives with MPD; therefore, three or four years are not that long to relearn, remember, regroup, and restart!

OUT OF MANY—ONE

Instead of relegating behavior and emotions and re-sponses to the multiple personalities that are part of her, the multiple will be able to respond as one person and one personality. She will remember people she has met each day, she will remember what she has done and said, and she will remember where she has parked her car because one personality will have done it all. The person with MPD can be encouraged that the disorder is treatable and that she will be able to reclaim her life.

The prognosis is good.

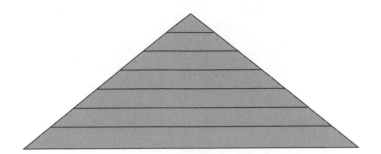

Section 4

HEALING

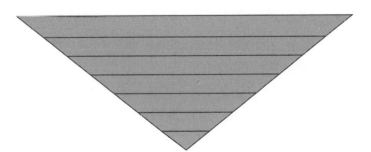

Chapter Fifteen

GOALS OF THERAPY

Once I have given a patient the diagnosis of multiple personality disorder, she has a great sense of relief that her problem has a name, an etiology, and a prognosis. She also has a sense of wonder and fear. She may ask herself, What is this disorder all about? Could I really have all those personalities inside me? It cannot be! Yet . . . this diagnosis finally makes sense. This diagnosis would certainly explain all the peculiarities of my life. Is it possible that someone with MPD can get over this disorder? Will I always be this way? Is there any hope for me?

One of the first misconceptions about the treatment of MPD is that therapy is supposed to make the alters disappear. That is not true. The multiple or family and friends or sometimes inexperienced therapists may think that if there were no alters switching in and out, that would take care of the problem. This idea reflects an incomplete understanding of the true nature of MPD and how it operates within the life of the patient as a coping mechanism.

To begin with, the alters have served a very specific

> *Instead of delegating her memories and responses to various alters, the patient with MPD must be taught to handle all of these responses and responsibilities herself.*

purpose and have been extremely important for the survival of the multiple. The goal of therapy is not to get rid of the alters per se but to teach the multiple to do for herself what the alters have been doing all along. Instead of delegating her memories and responses to various alters, the patient with MPD must be taught to handle all of these responses and responsibilities herself. She must learn to get angry and to be angry in an appropriate manner. She must stand up for herself, and she must express the full range of emotions that all of the alters have been doing for her.

To do this, the multiple will need to learn how to face the old painful memories and any new painful situations as *one person.* She will need to know the memories of one alter, handle the emotional reactions of another alter, and be able to respond as perhaps even another alter would, but she will need to do it all as one personality with full knowledge and forethought.

FOUR GOALS OF THERAPY

Within this understanding, there are several general and several specific goals of therapy for the person with MPD. The goal is *not* to erase the presence of the alters. One does not get rid of alters as one gets rid of warts. In the early historic stages of treatment of MPD, some therapists made that mistake. They managed to knock out some personalities (or at least made them disappear for a while) and declared the patient was "cured." Unfortunately, as they were to find out later, either the old alters returned, or other, newer personalities stepped in to take over those roles.

The overall goal of therapy is to stop the multiplicity. Instead of getting many alter personalities to respond to many different circumstances, the goal of therapy is to get one personality—the core personality—to respond to all circumstances. Out of many, we want one! Within this single overall goal, there are several specific goals:

1. To make the patient and the alters aware of the diagnosis and able to understand the disorder.

2. To enable the patient to respond out of the present instead of the past.

3. To allow the patient with multiple personality disorder to catch up with development.

4. To integrate the abilities and skills and talents of all of the alternate personalities so that one solid fused core personality will be available to respond, react, and remember.[1]

Let me break these points down a little more, so we can understand the components of the therapeutic goals in treating MPD.

The *first goal* of treatment is to make the patient and the alters aware of the diagnosis and able to understand the disorder. I do not give my patients their diagnosis the very first day that I suspect they have MPD. Depending on the personality, the emotional responses, the level of stability, and the level of trust they establish with me, I wait to see that they are really ready for the diagnosis. The life of a multiple can be up and down and at times multiples are very, very fragile people. I know that if I tell some of these patients before they are ready to handle the diagnosis, they may become overwhelmed and drop out of therapy altogether. Even patients who have been in and out of psychiatric hospitals—and have been diagnosed (or misdiagnosed) with every conceivable mental and physical illness under the sun—can find it overwhelming to be diagnosed with MPD.

Deep inside, they have awareness or knowledge that MPD is their actual problem. They are relieved to have a diagnosis, yet they fear the unknown. They are afraid of what MPD will mean in their everyday lives (even though they have been living with it since they were toddlers); they are afraid to tell their friends for fear of rejection; they are afraid of the treatment and what it might entail.

I also need to befriend and build trust with *the alters* and to reveal the diagnosis to them. Sometimes I can reveal the diagnosis to a strong alter, such as the rescuer, before I can tell the core personality. But all of the personalities need to be informed about the diagnosis and to understand what is expected in treatment.

The *second goal* of therapy is to enable the patient to respond out of the present instead of the past. Almost all of the pain and the emotional responses of the person with MPD are centered on the past life. The patient is constantly acting out today some aspect of experiences from *yesterday.* Painful emotions locked up in the alters' memories hold the patient hostage to the past through auditory, olfactory, and tactile memories. My patient Patricia, who was a victim of ritual abuse, was unable to continue preparing dinner because the smell of meat brought back too many terrifying memories from her childhood. The other patient, Charlene, was unable to build trust with anyone because she was still responding to the pain she felt as a toddler when her mother betrayed her emotionally, psychologically, and physically.

The *third goal* of treatment is to allow the patient with multiple personality disorder to catch up with development. In this capacity, I want to retrain the multiple to respond to circumstances the way other people usually do.

The memory bank needs to be retrained or reprogrammed. The multiple needs to remember and acknowledge the traumatic events that happened instead of keeping those memories split off and locked up with an alter. In the early childhood of the multiple, the traumas and abuses led to the first episodes of splitting and dissociation, and thus the creation of the first alters. All of the memories are in the mind—nothing is ever lost. However, the multiple has stored these memories in such a way that she has no access to them. The alters are the keepers of the memories.

To heal the effects of these traumatic events and to

> *Painful emotions locked up in the alters' memories hold the patient hostage to the past through auditory, olfactory, and tactile memories.*

put the memories into the consciousness of the core personality, the memories need to be *abreacted*. It is a reliving of the original event by reenacting (within the mind) the trauma. An abreactment involves total recall and sensation, both physically and emotionally. Another way of looking at abreaction is imagining a long-playing flashback accompanied by the physical sensations. Once the event is abreacted, it will become part of the core personality's conscious memory. Therapists often use hypnosis as the tool to access the memories of these first traumatic splitting episodes and the ensuing abreaction with an alter personality.

Another area in which the multiple needs to be re-trained is that of emotional response. After the patient has abreacted the trauma that led to the creation of an alter, the patient will be in a position to take over that alter's emotional responses.

My patient Helen was physically and sexually abused by her grandfather from the age of two. Shortly after her third birthday, she dissociated and created an alter, Angry One, to handle the pain and the punishment. From that point on, Angry One would come out to handle any angry feelings for Helen. When Helen was in the fifth grade, a classmate treated her rudely and unfairly. Although Helen should have been able to express her outrage, she switched out instead, and Angry One was the personality who dealt with the schoolmate.

Working with a hypnotherapist, Angry One was able to recall and abreact the original trauma. In the process, Helen was finally able to know consciously the source of her pain. With the healing of the memory came an ability to tap into feelings and emotions, too. After that, whenever she experienced a provoking situation, Helen was able to start answering to the angry feelings herself rather than always disappearing and having Angry One take over.

> *In final fusion, all of the personalities have been joined together so that there are no separate alter personalities.*

The *fourth goal* of treatment is to integrate the abilities and skills and talents of all of the alternate personalities so that one solid fused core personality will be available to respond, react, and remember. The ultimate goal of therapy is the integration and final fusion of all of the personalities. Although at times some of these terms are used almost interchangeably, they have specific meanings for professionals in mental health. *Integration* is the process by which all of the alters begin to be connected through shared memory and interaction; it is the preparation for the final fusion. *Fusion* is the actual joining up of two personalities, usually an alter personality to the core personality. In final fusion, all of the personalities have been joined together so that there are no separate alter personalities.

STEPS FOR INTEGRATION AND FUSION

The entire process of integration and fusion encompasses three steps over the course of therapy:

1. The therapist must be able to build a solid bond of trust with the multiple and all of her alter personalities before any therapeutic progress can be made. I would have to say that trust is the most vital component of the clinical relationship.

2. The core personality and the alters must agree on common goals and objectives for the good of the whole person. The therapist must first work to gain the trust and confidence of all of the alters. As individuals, they must be in agreement to some degree that the survival of the organism (that is, the multiple) is the most important goal.

3. Whenever possible, the alters need to become coconscious and then copresent. If you'll remember, coconsciousness is the ability of an alter to observe and

remember what another alter is doing when that second alter is out. There is an awareness of the other's thoughts and behavior. Copresence takes this ability one step further—an alter not only understands what the other is thinking but influences the other's behavior. They are not fused, but they are present as two different personalities simultaneously; they are able to think and act out together.

RESULTS TO EXPECT FROM THERAPY

Time. As Helen indicated in her story, one of the most noticeable changes that is apparent after fusion is the passage of time. The patient will find that time now marches to the same clock everyone else has. She will have far more hours every week or even every day, depending on how severe her disorder. There will be no more blank spells—her days and weeks and months will have continuity and coherence rather than confusion.

Memory. For the first time in her life, the fused patient has a memory. She knows about her past, and the memories of the present become ongoing. For instance, the patient will remember where she parked her car because she will be the one who parked it—not another personality! Neither will she be a prisoner to her daily lists because she will remember what she is doing and where she is going.

Control. The patient will have a far greater sense of control over her life. She will no longer find new clothes in her closet that she doesn't like and that she doesn't remember buying. She will no longer have strangers coming up and addressing her by different names. She can make plans for herself and for her life and know that they will come to pass because she is in control!

> *The successfully fused patient will have kept the best talents and capabilities of the alters but will be relieved of the blank spells and confusion.*

Appropriate emotional response. The patient will be able to overcome personal battles and tragedies on her own. She will take responsibility for her actions and will remember what she has done. Instead of either over-reacting or underreacting, she will confront difficulties and disappointments with the appropriate emotional responses, including anger, fear, sadness, happiness, joy, and confidence.

The successfully fused patient will have kept the best

talents and capabilities of the alters but will be relieved of the blank spells and confusion. The fully integrated patient will be ready to live as one person with one personality and a complete, mature complement of emotions and feelings and memories.

Chapter Sixteen

———

HEALING FOR INDIVIDUALS

When I have diagnosed patients as having MPD, I know they are going to be on my mind and on my heart. I know only too well that the extent of their injuries will go beyond the physical. I realize that they are feeling pain on all levels—consciously, unconsciously, and sub-consciously, and physically, spiritually, emotionally, and psychologically. For these reasons, patients with MPD cannot be compared to any other patients, nor can they be treated as such.

Because MPD is a coping mechanism and a learned response, it requires a multidimensional approach to be treated successfully. MPD is not an illness that can be treated or kept under control simply with a drug pre-scription; talk therapy is insufficient to handle the depth of injury and level of pain involved with patients with MPD.

My aim in multimodal therapy is to heal the patient effectively and efficiently wherever possible. I look at my patient in a holistic fashion—psychologically, neurophysiologically, biochemically, and spiritually. I want to tap into and heal the memories; I need to know the alters personally and how they contribute to and disrupt the system of the multiple; I want to help the patient sleep well at night to rest and rebuild. A multimodal therapeutic approach allows me to treat each patient with MPD as a unique person and to be able to consider the particular background and needs.

TOOLS

I use several therapeutic tools in working with patients with MPD. I am careful to individually adapt each tool to my patients. I stress this point because I must preserve the uniqueness of each patient, particularly those who are multiples. People with MPD are acutely aware of whether the therapist is really in tune to them.

If the psychiatrist has in mind a "one-size-fix-all" therapy or an assembly line approach to treatment, the multiple will be quick to sense it. The multiple wants to feel that she is being heard and understood and that her complaints are legitimate. How she is treated in therapy can either validate or undermine her fears and concerns about being in therapy.

The manner in which I use each tool depends on these factors: the nature and duration of the original abuse; the number and kinds of alters; the level of trust that I have built with the patient; the general health of the patient; and whether the patient is currently in a stable life-style situation.

For instance, a patient whose entire life has been deeply involved in a satanic cult will not require the same treatment given a multiple who was physically abused by her uncle for a five-year period. A patient who is now in an abusive marriage and out of a job will have different emotional needs than would a multiple who has a supportive, understanding spouse and a successful career.

Hypnosis

Hypnotherapy—the use of hypnosis in psychotherapy for patients with MPD—is the best available tool to uncover the significant history of the multiple. Hypnosis is used for the rapid collection of information and data. It allows the therapist to break through resistance and to bypass the usual long time period waiting for the multiple to try to consciously remember traumatic events. Sometimes, the patient remembers the event but is too emotionally disturbed by it to talk about it. A patient with a satanic ritual abuse background may be too afraid to talk about what she has experienced for fear of punishment or retribution.

Hypnotherapy is controversial. It has been an important tool for professionals in the field of psychotherapy when treating those with MPD. But some other therapists look upon hypnosis with a skeptical eye. There are three primary reasons for this hesitancy:

1. *History.* Hypnosis was first used as a method of treatment by the German physician Friedrich Mesmer (who called his treatment *mesmerism,* hence our word *mesmerize*). But associated with Mesmer and his treatment was the implication of magic, in particular, black magic. Therefore, some Christians feel that hypnotism has an unhealthy connection with evil rituals or that because of this connection, hypnotism is satanic in nature.

2. *Misuse.* Abuses have definitely occurred within the field of mental health involving hypnotism. Therapists with their own agendas have used hypnosis to try to get information about "past lives" of their patients or to "prove" reincarnation. This futile practice confuses the patient and can cause more harm. The hypnotist takes advantage of the heightened suggestibility of the patient when under hypnosis and then attempts to solicit information (as being factual) based on the given suggestions. I have also seen hypnosis misused in individuals with psychotic conditions such as schizophrenia where the patients are harmed rather than helped.

3. *Spirituality.* People (laypersons and cult members) have used hypnosis to introduce spiritual oppression or to subject the patient to evil influence, as witnessed by victims of satanic ritual abuse.

Despite these very real misuses, hypnosis can capably be a valid tool in the treatment of MPD. In the hands of a competent therapist, hypnosis brings about the rapid reorganization of memory that the *patient holds but has no access to.*

To begin with, *hypnosis* is the term for an extremely relaxed mental state, which is a dissociative state. If you remember my discussion of the drive I took from Santa Barbara to Los Angeles, that episode could be thought of as a slight state of dissociation. Hypnosis allows the subject to relax and have access to memories that may normally be blocked by cognitive dissonance. That is, a patient may be unable or unwilling to articulate the memories because she is embarrassed, greatly upset, or fearful. If the memories are sufficiently traumatic, the mind may have buried the memories at a very early age to protect the child.

Hypnosis also heightens suggestibility, which is why it can be tremendously helpful when used by a competent therapist (and can be harmful when deliberately misused). The therapist can make suggestions to the patient to help her relax or perhaps to help her overcome unnecessary fear about a particular event or person.

Everything that has happened to us as human beings —a spoken word or a sound we have heard, a flavor we have tasted, any event we have experienced, or anything we have seen—is there in the conscious and unconscious memory. Once imprinted, the memories are not "lost," even if we cannot remember them.

Brain surgeons have been fascinated to discover how competently and thoroughly the brain retains and stores these events. During brain surgery, physicians have found that when they lightly touch or stimulate different areas of the brain, the patient clearly remembers events that may have occurred years ago as a very young child. As the doctors touched different parts of the brain, the patient had different areas of memories—he could associate a particular smell with an event or a physical sensation. He was capable of remembering the most insignificant event, such as a birthday party attended at age five, with perfect clarity and complete recall.

For a patient with particularly painful memories that have been blocked from the conscious mind, hypnosis can reveal the memories of those events in a safer way to the therapist. In turn, the therapist can be more effective in treatment by knowing the underlying causes of the patient's disorder.

The therapist can arrange beforehand with the patient exactly what will and what will not be done, including all necessary precautions. For instance, the patient can ask the hypnotherapist to allow her to remember all of her session under hypnosis (as opposed to having the hypnotherapist reduce or affect her memory—"when you awaken, you will not remember any of this in your conscious memory").

> *Just as any tool can be used for beneficial purposes or misused for harmful purposes, hypnosis also has this capacity for health or harm.*

The point I would like to stress is that there is nothing inherently right or wrong about hypnosis. Just as any tool can be used for beneficial purposes or misused for harmful purposes, hypnosis also has this capacity for health or harm. For the vast majority of cases, however, it is a means to access memories, and in good hands it is an excellent therapeutic tool.

I make it a point to tell my patients that even while under a hypnotic trance they do not lose control of their will. They are free to disagree and refuse anything they find objectionable and may come out of the trancelike state if they desire.

Confidence and trust that the therapist will not violate this respect for the individual's choice is critical. One cannot be hypnotized against his or her will and cannot be forced to do anything under hypnosis that he or she opposes and chooses not to do. The therapist can make suggestions and even give directions, but the person's own will can override the suggestions if he or she so chooses.

When used this way, hypnotherapy is not a process of giving up control of one's own life to someone else's will. The therapeutic journey is a joint one, with the patient and therapist seeking the aforementioned goals.

A competent, caring, and communicative therapist who respects the patient and all of his or her rights, can be the best insurance to obtaining a good outcome.

Journaling

A therapist can't easily determine what events or people or stimuli in day-to-day living will cause a multiple to dissociate into an alternate personality, and what will cause the alter to switch into another personality. The core personality has no memory of any of these events, and the alters may or may not realize what was troubling for them, either! Multiples do not always feel comfortable verbalizing what is on their minds because they learned at such an early age that it is not safe to reveal secrets. Writing, on the other hand, allows them to reveal what is on their minds in a safe manner. Writing follows the letter of the law by not actually telling anyone, although perhaps not the spirit of the law because the writing is providing information to an outsider.

Journaling—keeping a regular log of events and thoughts on a day-to-day basis—provides the therapist with a tool to monitor the thought processes and behavior and reactions of the patient. It can be used to peek inside the mind. A journal can become a launching point for further discussion when dealing with shy or timid personalities: "I noticed in your journal, Anne, that you were very upset that Mrs. Rathbone called. Did she say something that bothered you, or is she still a reminder of those painful events?"

> *A journal can become a launching point for further discussion when dealing with shy or timid personalities.*

People with MPD are extraordinarily creative, so the journal becomes an outlet for expression and imagery. Patients often draw pictures and write poems, which can be extremely revealing of the patients and their alters. Journals allow the alters to see how the others feel and how they all fit and work inside the system. Sometimes, I see pictures of abuse or elements of satanic rituals drawn by the child alters. I also use them as discussion points: "Tell me about this picture. What is happening here to you?"

I like for my patients to keep journals because I can see the progress between sessions. If a patient had a particularly significant session (e.g., perhaps I revealed the diagnosis of multiple personality disorder to the patient, or the patient abreacted an important episode of abuse), I want to know the thoughts and emotions and reactions of the personalities to this session. How did they feel about the revelation of the diagnosis? What did the alters think about the core personality? Journals are one way to gain access to these intimate emotions.

Journals sometimes turn out to be diagnostic tools. As we saw in the case of MarieElena, I was able to use the journal writings to uncover a patient with MPD. The most obvious clue would be extreme variances in expression coupled with significant handwriting changes. Another possible indicator of MPD would be the content of the journal—pictures of torture or disturbing thought patterns might lead me to at least suspect childhood abuse.

Linda began to see a psychologist, Jim, for depression. Jim was a very sensitive, caring person and a thorough technician. He began to suspect MPD, and knowing of my work with patients in this arena, he asked me to give an evaluation as well.

In reviewing the patient's journal, I saw that many of her entries were symptomatic of classic depression. Her handwriting did not demonstrate extremes. However, some of Linda's references to "we" and to herself in the third person, as well as being overwhelmed by thoughts and voices, made me consider that hers could be a case of MPD.

When I combined what I had been reading in the journals with what I had observed in our few sessions and had noted in Linda's history, I suspected MPD. A diagnosis would never be made on the basis of the journal itself, but the journal provided clues to be further investigated and tested. In this sample of Linda's journal are references to the group and to "she":

> I'm drowning in my own thoughts . . . but there is no one to save me, my own thoughts are killing me . . . a slow agonizing death. Why shouldn't I just end it now? Come on you can do it if—
> no she can't!
> yes she can!
> no she can't!
> LEAVE ME ALONE
> **ALL OF YOU JUST SHUT UP**—I can't even think straight—
> **I just want to be normal!**

Another entry shows an altar with the word *RED* in heavy lettering. I suspected that Red was the name of an important persecutor alter, who was responsible for the cutting that Linda did to her body. I wondered if the mind was making a pun of the idea of having an *alter* on an *altar*. I noted throughout the journal that Linda referred to cutting herself and using pieces of sharp plastic and razors. Her discussion of cutting alerted me to consider that dissociation was taking place:

> RED is here but he's not cutting right now. He's protecting the others. There is such confusion and I am really scared again.

The monotone voices have set in and now there is such
confusion in my head.
There is a battle for my life and a
battle for my death.
If I stay here for tomorrow
then what do I have left?
A hollow shell of body
an empty, ashen curl
all the more appropriate
for a dead and deadly girl

As Jim, the psychologist, began unraveling more of
the history and other clues about Linda, the journal writings indicate that the multiple system was becoming
anxious that the secret would be let out:

After I cut my ankle, I thought about how would I hide
it from Jim. With this heat wave, I'll have to wear shorts
or a skirt and I'm afraid that he will see my ankle. I
played around with the scar and tried to rough up the
skin so it looks like a bad scrape.

He cannot find out because if he does, he will be watching us like a hawk and we need our secrets, so he cannot know. No one is going to close in on us, not even
him. There is no safe place now, not one.

It's all his fault. If it weren't for him, we'd be fine and
then he had to come along and start to mess with her
mind, he is going to mess up everything!

He is digging and probing and it is just a matter of time
that we are going to be found out. Get . . . out of her
life. YOU CAN'T FIND US . . . NO YOU CAN'T. Everything was fine, just leave us alone. . . .

To the secret place we must go,
away to a place far away
where no one will know
to the secret places we must go
where the pain is so sweet
and the scars in a row,
no one will find us,
no one will know.
We are in this together
forever and ever.

In this entry, the references to "we" and "her" and especially the panic expressed at having Jim discover who they are and what the secret is made me feel that it was written by one of the alters. One guess might be Red or another persecutor alter who was obviously doing more cutting. The phrase "safe place" is often used by adults who were sexually abused as children.

Mapping

Each alter has a very specific role tied to the emotional and physical well-being of the person with MPD. Ultimately, the alternate personalities are related to the core personality by either *emotion or event.* Drawing a map of these personalities is one way to get a look at the family system of the patient with MPD.

Without restricting the patient to a particular format, I ask the patient (or sometimes one of the alters) to write down the names of all of the alters and arrange them in any manner that is personally meaningful. Sometimes, these personalities are arranged in a chronology according to the age of the core personality when the alter was first "born." They could also be arranged in age order of

Drawing a map of the alternate personalities is one way to get a look at the family system of the patient with MPD.

the alters. I create my own maps of the personality systems to indicate which alters have information about or control an area that I am working in with the patient.

Chronology

Sometimes, the map indicates the chronological arrival of the alters—who first appeared on the scene to rescue the multiple when she was three years old, who was created when she was eight, and so on. That gives me information about how long these personalities have been affecting the life of the multiple.

A Chronological Map of Alters

(Age of Core Personality When Alter First Appeared)

Early Life	Teen Years	Twenties
Freddie at age 2½	William the Conqueror at age 13	Vidal at age 26
Big Jim at age 4		
Scarface at age 5	Vanessa at age 15	
Grandmother at age 5	St. David at age 15	

David—the Core Personality (34 years old)

Relationship Clusters

Another arrangement concerns relationship clusters between alters. Several may be related because they deal with various interpretations of an emotion. For instance, one alter may act out when he is angry. By acting out, I mean that this alter uses aggressive behavior toward others. He will fight, strike back at another, swear, steal, destroy, and so on. Another alter may act in when she feels angry. She swallows the anger and allows it to fester inside, she takes out her feelings of frustration and unexpressed anger on herself. This alter will cut herself, take drugs, or engage in other self-endangering behavior. So we can see that these two alters may have different ways of expressing the emotions of anger and rage, but they are related in that both are responsible for handling the pent-up angry feelings for the multiple system.

A Relationship Map of Alters

(How Alters Are Related Through Emotions)

Anger/Fear

Scarface will act out, fight, and swear

Freddie will cry, run away, and hide

Vanessa will act in, become depressed and despondent

William the Conquerer excels at a challenge, is energized with adrenaline, and will take drugs

David—The Core Personality

Functions and Roles

Maps can portray the functions and roles of the alters within the personality system, allowing the therapist to identify the troublemakers as well as the possible allies.

Healing for Individuals

A Map of Alters and Their Functions

(How Alters Are Related Through Roles)

Persecutor

Scarface is aggressive, physically strong, violent

Vanessa takes drugs and holds memories of much of the sexual abuse

Sheila is a cult informer created by the cult to respond on cue

Uncle is critical and abusive of the host, the embodiment of a former perpetrator

Child Alter

Freddie has memory for being bad and holds (took) the physical abuse

Protector

Big Jim protects with physical behavior

Vidal is a diplomat

Grandmother soothes

St. David is deeply religious and will pray about everything; holds on to hope

David—The Core Personality

Communication Systems

Mapping may indicate which alters know or are aware of other alters. If you remember, some alters are amnesiac to other alters; some are copresent or cocognizant. This map helps me because as I am talking to one alter, I know which other alters are able to "listen in." I can take advantage of this unique situation by having to give my information only once while the others are listening. Sometimes I talk to one alter, giving suggestions about how to improve her relationship with another, say, a persecutor. I refer to the absent persecutor alter and discuss her behavior in such a way that it will provide a positive message, knowing that the persecutor is hearing everything I am saying!

Here is what I might say when I know I am dealing with alters in this capacity: "Christine, I know that Godiva's behavior is really disturbing all of you. But it might help all of you to understand Godiva better if you could remember that she is really only looking for attention when she goes out to bars. I think if you all could give her more attention and treat her with respect, she may not feel such an intense need to go out and prove herself to men. Perhaps Godiva does not know that the children [Timmy and Little Carleen] find her behavior very scary for them. She is very compassionate with little children and probably doesn't realize that her actions frighten them when they switch out and find themselves with these angry men."

I knew from the mapping work I had done with my patient Carla and with her alter Christine that Godiva wasn't "connected" with anyone. She was not related within the system by either emotion or function. And I also knew that she was cocognizant with Christine (she could see and hear everything that Christine did). Armed with this knowledge and sensing that Godiva was terribly fond of the little children, I purposely gave this information to Christine in my session with her. I knew that Godiva would overhear all of it, and I hoped she would be able to start to act on these suggestions.

Medicine

In an era of natural healing and organic, holistic treatments, people tend to downplay the importance of medicine and to view prescriptions with a negative eye. I understand the concern because drugs and pharmaceuticals have been overused and misused. As a specialist in psychopharmacology, however, I have been able to observe firsthand the benefits of medical research applied to the suffering and pain in human life. Medicine is like the other tools we have discussed in that when it is utilized correctly, it can be a boon and a blessing for the patient.

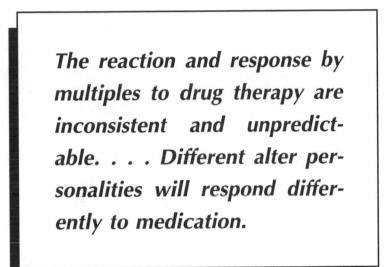

The reaction and response by multiples to drug therapy are inconsistent and unpredictable. . . . Different alter personalities will respond differently to medication.

When dealing with MPD from a medication standpoint, physicians are in a brand-new ballpark. The reaction and response by multiples to drug therapy are inconsistent and unpredictable. Some obvious peculiarities of the disorder will distort or dismiss the usual precautions taken in prescribing medication. To begin with, I've noticed that there is no such thing as a standard dosage for people with MPD. Some of the multiples I've treated have required extraordinarily high dosages to gain relief.

Prescriptions must be made for whomever has executive control of the body; however, a different alter who switches out will then be under the influence of the drug. Different alter personalities will respond differently to medication. A prescription that is therapeutic for one alter may have more adverse effects on another. An adult dosage would be too much for a child alter who switches out during the course of medication.

Therefore, I try to take reasonable precautions before prescribing medication. I ask some of these questions:

- What are the possibilities for abuse or intentional misuse of the drug by some of the disruptive or persecutor alters?

- What are the potential side effects if overdosed?

- What is the status of the overall system? Is this a new patient? Does she have a fairly stable system?

- Are there any other modes of therapy that could bring about the same effect without medication?

- Do any of the alter personalities have a problem with drug or alcohol abuse or dependency?

- Will the majority of the personalities benefit from the medication? I would hesitate to prescribe any medication that would be therapeutic for only one or two personalities because of possible side effects to other alters.

- Overall, would the patient be better off with or without medication?

In general, I prescribe medication when I notice that sleep deprivation or extreme anxieties and stress are robbing the physical body of much-needed rest. Mild tranquilizers on a short-term basis are effective, yet I have to carefully monitor the patient for physiological or psychological dependency.

Some patients will experience extreme anxiety during crucial periods of adjustment within the course of therapy. These flashpoints are examples:

1. Revelation of diagnosis

2. Major abreactions or other breakthrough revelations

3. Final stages of fusion

Dysphoria (sadness) is a very common experience among multiples and/or their alters; it is generally not a complaint to be taken too seriously in and of itself. However, if the entire system becomes too overwhelmed by depression, I try medication to stabilize the personalities.

The headaches that are a frequent complaint among people with MPD do not respond well to medication. I can try to help the patient with relaxation techniques, but usually, these headaches are related to the phenomenon of switching between personalities.

Hearing voices does not go away with the use of antipsychotic drugs, nor do the other forms of tactile or olfactory hallucinations and memories commonly seen in MPD. The use of antipsychotic medications in small dosages, however, may be helpful in reducing the intensity in patients for whom the experiences are extremely disruptive. Sometimes, however, I have seen patients react unfavorably with increased fear to this category of medications. Careful dosing, thorough monitoring, and close follow-up will help to prevent this type of problem and ensure a more desirable effect of medication usage.

Various categories of medications may be prescribed alone or in combination with one another. None can "cure" MPD. The goal of medication is to reduce the intensity of the various symptoms that patients may experience related to the disorder and above all keep them safe. Because of the special considerations in MPD, medication regimens must be uniquely tailored and closely monitored.

Group Therapy

Because of the uniqueness of MPD, some standard treatments appropriate to other mental or psychological conditions may not be appropriate for multiples or must be adjusted to fit the complexities involved. I have one precaution and one promotion for group therapy as a therapeutic approach for those with MPD.

First, the precaution. In general, group therapy is not effective for multiples if they are being placed in a mixed patient setting, that is, a general group therapy session involving multiples and nonmultiple patients. For instance, an unstable alcoholic alter may not do well going to a meeting of other drug abusers. In most group therapy sessions that allowed multiples, the therapy was not effective for the following reasons:

- The multiples tended to dominate the group discussion.

- Alters kept flitting in and out (much to the amazement and confusion of the nonmultiple patients).

- The therapists spent too much time counseling the multiples during the session.

- The nonmultiples resented the multiples for presenting a "more-abused-than-thou" story. Although each patient had a problem childhood, the nonmultiples were left feeling that their problems were made insignificant when compared to those of the multiples.

That being said, group therapy may be appropriate in some cases:

- The sessions can have mixed patients—multiples and nonmultiples—provided there is a strong correlating factor. I would suggest having adult survivors of childhood sexual abuse—in particular, incest.

- The multiples should be far enough along in therapy to be very stable (no alters jumping in and out) and should be carefully screened before being allowed to enter group therapy.

- All participants must be willing to respect total confidentiality for all information presented during the sessions.

- The sessions need to be led by very strong and very secure therapists. They need to be able to control the alters from dominating and switching too often.

If the ground rules are carefully laid out and adhered to, and the patients (both multiple and nonmultiple) are carefully screened, group therapy may be beneficial for mature multiple patients. It provides them with new information about behavior and relationships. It is healthy for a multiple to see how incest affects a nonmultiple patient. The multiple sees that the nonmultiple shares a common problem—incest—and is also deeply affected by this issue, yet does not utilize dissociation and alter personalities as coping mechanisms. The group therapy sessions can substantiate for the multiple information given by her individual therapist about "normal" behavior, problem solving, and relationships. And a place of acceptance and shared experience (albeit traumatic) is very helpful in providing the multiple with a sense of stabilization and of not being alone in life.

> *A team can conquer some very tough cases that would overwhelm many therapists acting alone.*

SUMMARY

The complexity of this disorder requires a complex mixture of therapies. Some are more successful than others, and they must be adjusted to meet the specific needs of each new case. So much is required to deliver the care in so many diverse forms that some therapists do not have the time to do an adequate job. Many therapists start strong only to find themselves burned out and resentful. A better solution is to have a team approach in the treatment. A team can conquer some very tough cases that would overwhelm many therapists acting alone.

If you are a therapist treating MPD patients, frequent consultation and collaboration with colleagues experienced in this area can be invaluable. Working with a team can provide this and allow for collateral support for patients when you are unavailable or on vacation.

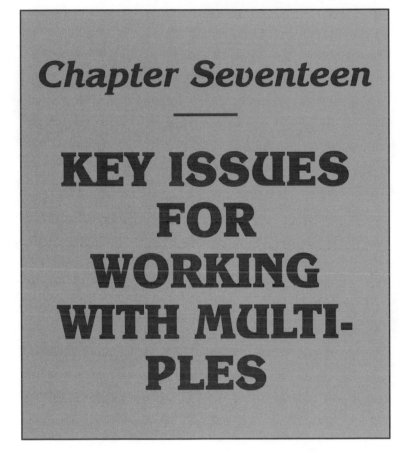

Chapter Seventeen

KEY ISSUES FOR WORKING WITH MULTI-PLES

As we approach the end of the twentieth century, we become increasingly knowledgeable about the world around us, and at the same time, we become increasingly aware of *how little we really do know!* In the field of mental health, we have made considerable gains in understanding and treating numerous mental illnesses and psychological disorders. Yet as we start to deal with the complexities of multiple personality disorder, we can see that we are just beginning to comprehend how the mind and the body work together.

Although major studies and research on MPD are in the infancy stages, I feel that it is important for everyone to be educated on what is known. Some cynics feel that this disorder's increasing prevalence is undeserving— perhaps too many therapists are too quick to suspect and diagnose MPD. I would encourage people to remember that the disorder has always been with us; only the correct diagnosis has been increasing, not necessarily the incidence of MPD. Since numerous studies have indicated that the average multiple has been in the mental health system for at least five years with at least two wrong diagnoses, I think research bears out my claim.

If it is still difficult for mental health professionals to understand and accept a diagnosis of MPD, we can well

> *Numerous studies have indicated that the average multiple has been in the mental health system for at least five years with at least two wrong diagnoses.*

imagine the confusion among other professions when faced with those challenged by the disorder. For instance, many thorny questions have been raised by the legal field and law enforcement agencies. If those of us in mental health are still confused or in disagreement about MPD, the rest of the world will have a much greater problem with the disorder.

I would like to address some of the concerns and problems of other professionals and laypersons in dealing with MPD.

HEALTH CARE PROFESSIONALS

One key step in the healing and recovery of persons with MPD is the early detection and treatment of those at risk for the disorder. That is why I feel it is so crucial for *all* health professionals to be well aware, well read, and well educated on the subject of MPD. In particular, I want to stress that pediatricians should become informed on the subject to identify young children who might be at risk for MPD.

Researchers think that as many as one-fourth of severely abused children could potentially develop MPD. Pediatricians should be alerted not only to signs of abuse but also to unusual behavior or complaints. For instance, a pediatrician who suspects any at-risk family settings (cult worshipers or multigeneration sexual abuse) should be on the lookout for corresponding manifestations in the child's behavior or on the body.

Some of these might include the following:

- Unusual fears (e.g., ropes, sheets, Jacuzzis, toilets)

- Bizarre topics of conversation (e.g., "black and candles all around"; "they make me eat the poopoo and the peepee")

- Bizarre self-abuse (e.g., cutting, burning body parts)

- Sexualization of neutral objects, especially if the child refers to "sticks" or snakes being inserted in body parts

- Vocabulary that alludes to satanic themes (e.g., "sacrifice" or "married to the evil one")

LAW ENFORCEMENT AND FORENSIC ISSUES

Issues involving MPD have increasingly become a concern in the legal system. The law—as it stands now—can make no provisions for a disorder that is only barely understood by mental health itself. Three famous cases during the last ten years included two defendants who claimed MPD as a defense. Billy Milligan was accused of raping two women, and Kenneth Bianchi, the "Hillside Strangler," was accused of raping and murdering thirteen young women.

The issue is further complicated in that professionals who would be sufficiently knowledgeable about the disorder to make a diagnosis in a defendant would probably disagree that it should be labeled an insanity defense! Because of the unique aspects of MPD, it defies the usual categorizations.

Then, too, an unknowledgeable public finds the disorder, and especially the defense, highly suspect. Much about MPD as it is exhibited behaviorally looks like ordinary criminal behavior.

Criminal Behavior	*Multiple Personality Behavior*
The suspect lies.	The multiple is amnesiac for behavior of an alter and lies to cover up.
The suspect is manipulative.	Suicide, cutting, and self-mutilation may appear manipulative, and are common.

The suspect has aliases.	The multiple has different alters with different names.
The suspect steals.	The multiple finds an object, which was bought or brought in by an alter to the multiple personality. Some alters practice deviant, antisocial behaviors.
The suspect evades the authorities.	The multiple is overwhelmed by a distressing event, and an alter takes over and leaves. The multiple appears elusive.

Primarily, the public is worried that offenders will try to use MPD as an excuse to get off the hook. But again, I strongly state the reminder that we far more often *overlook* rather than *overdiagnose* the problem. Generally, the defense of MPD is dismissed because it is too difficult to comprehend and explain to a jury.

Chris Sizemore, herself a fused and integrated multiple who was the subject of *The Three Faces of Eve,* reviewed tapes showing Kenneth Bianchi and concluded that he was a fake. Cornelia Wilbur, who treated Sybil and is one of the foremost authorities on MPD, met with Billy Milligan and diagnosed him as definitely having the disorder. I believe that those who have dealt extensively with the disorder on a firsthand basis should work more closely with persons in law enforcement—to educate officials on the nature of the disorder *before* a case pops up and then to work with them in verifying a diagnosis afterward. Primarily, I see that the law in this

> *Generally, the defense of MPD is dismissed because it is too difficult to comprehend and explain to a jury.*

area is still very new and will become established only as clinicians are further educated and convinced of the diagnosis. Another area of potential legal concern with multiples is informed consent. Is it possible to get consent from all the alters? No, especially in the beginning of treatment.

HOSPITAL AND INPATIENT STAFF

Although people involved in hospital and inpatient care are primarily well-meaning, sensitive individuals dedicated to the well-being of their patients, they have at times done disservice to patients with MPD. There are three troublesome areas in regard to hospital personnel and multiples:

1. The hospital personnel may not believe the diagnosis and may refuse to deal with the patient in any special manner. Most often, the multiple is in the psychiatric ward, and the staff are used to mental patients lying and fabricating stories to get attention. If a patient claims she is a multiple and the staff are not familiar with the

disorder, they may assume it is another ruse by the patient to get special favors or manipulate them.

A mental patient could possibly fake the disorder. However, if a patient claims to be a multiple, it is important *to listen to the nature of her requests and complaints in regard to this diagnosis.* In other words, looking beyond her claim that she is a multiple, what is the point that she is trying to make?

If she is not a multiple, there is still a need to evaluate her claims including that she may be looking for attention. If she is a multiple, she may be sufficiently knowledgeable about her condition to be concerned about her health and safety.

For instance, when the patient says she is a multiple and insists that she is not a schizophrenic and asks to not be given any drugs to treat psychosis, she may know what she is talking about. The staff member might ask the patient how she knows her diagnosis. The staff member could confirm if the patient is or was in therapy by calling the therapist.

> *Multiples are terrified of hospitals and being locked up.*

2. The patient may be frequently out of control, acting out, disruptive, and sometimes violent. Multiples are terrified of hospitals and being locked up. Hospitals repre-

sent pain and control by others—two familiar and uncomfortable issues with multiples. Therefore, if or when a patient with MPD is put into an inpatient situation, she will become frightened and overwhelmed, and many of the alters will start switching out in response to her, or their own, anxieties.

Some of the alters may be children who cry and throw tantrums. Other alters may be persecutors who bully or attack staff when perceiving a threat.

If the patient knows that she is a multiple, the staff should learn which alters to call upon when things get out of control and how to call them. When she is far enough along in therapy, the multiple may help the staff in identifying people, objects, or activities that are most likely to make any of the personalities in the system feel anxious or threatened.

3. The hospital staff may accept the diagnosis too well. Sometimes, certain hospital personnel's acceptance of MPD can become unproductive for the patient. The staff may treat the patient as a curiosity and repeatedly ask the patient to switch into other alters, which demeans and depersonalizes the multiple and the alters. And some of the alters may take advantage of the fascination and curiosity of the staff to manipulate them. That can really become a problem if the entire staff do not agree about the diagnosis. The nonbelievers will resent the attention and time spent by the nurses and aides in accommodating special needs by the patient with MPD.

FOR FAMILIES OF A PATIENT
WITH MPD

The diagnosis of multiple personality disorder for a loved one can be both overwhelming and frightening. It is overwhelming because the family does not know what to expect: What does the diagnosis mean? What will treatment entail? Sometimes there is anger at the therapist for suggesting such a diagnosis. The diagnosis is frightening because to the family, MPD suggests something unpleasantly bizarre, perhaps inhuman. The family is insulted that such a phenomenon could be taking place among its ranks.

In other cases, the diagnosis is a major relief. The family may have suspected all along that something was askew but did not have the capacity to figure out exactly what was wrong. In these cases, the diagnosis makes sense of seemingly senseless incidents and behavior. It is a satisfactory explanation, and although the concept may be difficult for children, they are surprisingly often the most accepting.

The very best and very first thing a family should do upon confirming the diagnosis is to educate themselves about the disorder. At the end of this book, you'll find a list of many excellent books about the disorder, ranging from biographies to books about treatment by therapists. There are also a number of support groups throughout the nation as well as newsletters and resources for families and friends of patients with the disorder. (See "Resources" section.)

My suggestion to both the patient and to the family is that it is not necessary to tell anyone about the diagnosis. The patient can afford to be cautious because so many people have no knowledge or have gross misconceptions about MPD and they may reject the patient. I feel that the patient can usually trust her best instincts about which friends to tell and when to tell them.

A WORD FOR THERAPISTS

Even though a successfully integrated multiple is a vastly rewarding aspect of treatment for any therapist, the process can be demanding and exhausting. Whether the therapist takes a "professional only" stance (seeing the patient at prearranged meetings in an office setting) or whether the therapist decides to nurture a patient and go on excursions outside the office, it will be difficult to avoid overinvolvement with the patient at some point along the therapeutic road. To remain sensitive but avoid overinvolvement is a must for both the patient's and the therapist's sake.

A therapist who is in it for the long haul might consider working closely with a cotherapist in treating a patient with MPD. There can be great support, mutual exchange of ideas on treatment and procedures with two therapists. One can take notes and observe while the other conducts the session. One therapist can substitute if another begins to feel emotionally overwhelmed. The patient is less likely to take advantage of or to be able to manipulate both therapists. As a psychiatrist, I often work in collaboration with therapists who are also treating the patient.

The therapist must keep abreast of developments in the field and get the support and exchange of other therapists working with MPD across the nation. An international organization is devoted to dissociative disorders—the International Society for the Study of Multiple Personality and Dissociation. (Information about the organization and its newsletter is included in the "Resources" section.)

CLERGY

I finish here with an address to the clergy because they can round out a successful treatment program for the person with MPD.

Individuals who work in Christian counseling or are involved in any way with the psychological welfare of another need to remain sensitive to the possibility of encountering a patient with MPD. If they would familiarize themselves with its unique symptoms, they would be in a better position to identify a patient with the disorder rather than give a misdiagnosis of spiritual possession.

On the other hand, the clergy can gain the trust of a ritual abused alter or multiple more quickly because those in Christian counseling are far more accepting and knowledgeable about spiritual warfare. The clergy may be in the best position to provide full recovery not only because they are more likely to perform exorcisms when needed but because they recognize the power of prayer. As a patient moves to final fusion and is wrapping up the division of thought and behavior, memory and emotions, a clergy member can offer healing and peace leading to wholeness that can come only through prayer and spiritual intervention.

Chapter Eighteen

———

OF GOD AND EVIL

I was working at the Azusa New Life Treatment Center when a new employee, just out of school with a degree in psychology, wanted to talk about what it was like working in the real world of providing psychiatric care to some very troubled people. She had been there about six weeks, and the predictable glassy-eyed expression had set in from being astonished day after day by incredibly complex patient after patient. The discussions were common because most schools do not adequately prepare a master's level person for the crises encountered in an acute psychiatric setting. What we do in the hospital is nothing like an outpatient practice, for which most training is directed. With patients staying at the hospital twenty-four hours a day, it is difficult to hide what could be covered up in a one-hour session at a counseling center. As a result, the new employees are usually amazed at how little they know, how complicated treatment can be, and how wonderful the results can be for most who come for help.

On that morning, the discussion did not center on the traditional talk of psychiatry, psychological theory, or an aspect of a patient's treatment. The discussion was about something much more important than Sigmund Freud when it comes to treating multiple personalities.

Like me, the student was a Christian, and she stated something that I believe very firmly. She said, "This is not just treating emotional problems. This is spiritual warfare!" To some people, spiritual warfare may sound more like voodoo than proper treatment for someone in a psychiatric hospital, but I can assure you, those who do not understand the spiritual battle that is being waged in the life of a multiple will not be able to fully help that person regain a full, meaningful life with purpose.

> *When working with multiples, it requires a keen understanding of both the spiritual and the scientific.*

We are living in a post-Christian era where almost anything that has to do with Christianity or traditional faith is viewed as nothing more than old-time religion. That is truer in the scientific community than anywhere else. All scientific study is conducted to understand the reality of things that are observable and measurable in the here and now. Issues of faith and spirituality deal with things that are often not measurable or observable and place more emphasis on the hereafter rather than the here and now! Science deals with the absolutes, the facts, the events in the universe, the verifiable happenings supported by cold, hard data and warm-blooded witnesses. On the other hand, the spiritual deals with our *interpretation* of these events in the universe and what they mean to each of us personally on an eternal dimension. The split between these two areas is clear and distinct, but when working with multiples, it requires a keen understanding of both the spiritual and the scientific. The treatment must adhere to the highest levels of quality clinical care and at the same time address the underlying spiritual issues involved in the development of the problem and the process of overcoming and reintegration.

Although a split between mental health and religion exists today, there was a time when issues of spirituality, psychology, emotional well-being, and mental state were more closely connected. Dr. Ralph Allison addresses this point in his book on multiple personality disorder titled *Minds in Many Pieces:*

> It is important to remember that religion and mental health are not as contradictory as they may seem. In earlier times, the church cared for the mentally ill. The fact that doctors have taken over this function doesn't mean that bringing religion to a treatment program is wrong. Essentially, I was bringing mental health full circle, combining the best of medicine and religion. Since my family has produced a long line of ministers, it seemed quite natural for me to mix a religious act with

my psychiatry since this seemed to be in the best interest of my patient.[1]

This issue is not just vital for the psychologist; it is
also essential for the minister since both professions
have in the past done so poorly at working with persons
who have multiple personalities. The minister refusing
to look at the psychological dimensions of the problem
is just as constrained as the psychologist refusing to look
at the spiritual dimensions. Both will do a disservice to
the treatment of multiples if they do not consider the
truth that is known from the other perspective, whether
it is psychological or spiritual.

Dr. Allison is a good example of the attitude needed
when faced with poor results based on traditional treatment approaches: "Despite my skepticism at the time, I
believed then and still believe that a good psychiatrist
must be open to new ideas. The welfare and eventual
cure of the patient must be his only consideration, and
when conventional techniques fail, he must be willing
to explore new options."[2]

BACK TO THE BIBLE

As a clinician, I rely on my training and new research
presented in the journals of my profession. But another
source, a greater, more important source, gives me a
solid foundation and understanding for everything I read
and observe. That source is the Bible. I really do believe
the Bible is the Word of God. I believe He inspired the
writers and within the Book is timeless divine wisdom.
This book provides a clear understanding of several aspects of MPD that remain a mystery to most in the psy-

chiatric profession. When the new graduate declared that working with multiple personalities involved spiritual warfare, she had concluded in six weeks what many of our greatest minds will never understand or accept.

In the New Testament of the Bible, there is a letter written to the church members in the town of Ephesus. The letter, written by the apostle Paul, is called Ephesians. One special verse offers insight for anyone treating multiple personalities: "For we do not wrestle against flesh and blood, but against principalities, against powers, against the rulers of the darkness of this age, against spiritual hosts of wickedness in the heavenly places" (6:12).

When I am with a person with MPD, I think of the things of God and the things of evil that may be influencing the person. I think of the satanic ritual abuse that often starts the splitting process and the evil of these cults. I think of how they are so skilled at destroying persons, cutting them off from themselves, segmenting them into fragments. When I begin the process of reintegration, I think on these things because I know that while I am providing clinical care, a spiritual battle with the forces of evil is also being conducted for the heart of my patient.

To fight this battle, I have tools at my disposal that go beyond what I learned in my clinical training. In the same letter to the Ephesians, Paul talked about these tools, which are available for anyone who is a believer. Anyone working with someone who has been involved with the occult and satanic ritual abuse must be equipped with the full armor that God provides. Truth, righteousness, and readiness are essentials. There is so much deception in working with people with MPD that we must always be dedicated to knowing the truth and remain deeply rooted in God's truth. We need to be righteous people. There are so many temptations that if we do not have personal integrity, we may get trapped in unhealthy relationships or be tempted to attempt a quick fix for something that requires long-term treatment. We must be ready for anything and surprised at nothing. Our attitude of readiness allows us to meet the patient's needs. This attitude motivates us to go the extra distance and exert the extra effort required in successful MPD treatment.

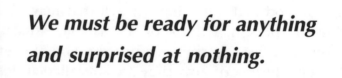

> *We must be ready for anything and surprised at nothing.*

In another letter to another church, Paul wrote, "For though we walk in the flesh, we do not war according to the flesh. For the weapons of our warfare are not carnal but mighty in God for pulling down strongholds" (2 Cor. 10:3-4). Restated in this context, those of us on the treatment team do not use only the tools we learned in school or the ideas we get out of journals; we call on God to assist us with His divine power to remove the barriers to reintegration. This perspective gives us a strong foundation with greater optimism for the patient's full reintegration and ability to function as a healthy human being.

This perspective also affords us the opportunity to win a patient's confidence sooner. Someone talking about satanic ritual abuse and the forces of evil will often be disbelieved in the secular psychiatric setting, even if it can be proven that the perpetrators of abuse were known cult members. A patient fears revealing the details of abuse because she senses that she is not being believed and her credibility is being questioned. Rapport breaks down, and the therapeutic process stops. Believing in the existence of evil and understanding the powers at war for the soul of the patient allow us to see the patient as a credible witness to her abuse and the subsequent adjustments made in an attempt to cope.

THE TOOLS

In an attempt to treat the person with MPD with quality clinical care while addressing the spiritual aspects of the problem, treatment utilizes tools that would not be accepted as valid in some psychiatric circles. These tools enable the staff to meet the needs of the multiple in a comprehensive plan addressing every aspect of the problem. These tools are used in addition to those used in most psychiatric settings, such as group and individual therapy.

Prayer is the most powerful tool in dealing with multiples. The staff pray for each other, and we pray for patients. This prayer gives us a common bond with each other and the patients while calling upon the power of God to help us as we attempt to help. It also has a calming and relaxing effect on the patients as they sense that the struggle to reintegrate will not be carried out alone, that God will assist them in every step. We have sccn wonderful results, and we attribute much of this success to the power of prayer.

Bible study is another valuable tool for patients. When they read the Bible, they read about everything from demon possession to people with severe emotional problems. These stories reflect the power of God to deal with even the most evil and destructive forces. Patients are comforted to know that they have hope to be free, and the Bible stories are a witness to people making miraculous changes.

The study of the Bible can also help patients see that what has often been labeled possession by the church is really something quite different. We can point to stories such as the one where demons were cast out into a herd of pigs and show how different that was from what patients experience. We can separate reality from a pseudospiritual approach to all problems. Our using the Bible shows Christian patients that we embrace its truth, but we also know that some have misinterpreted the Bible and that misinterpretation has been harmful.

As a Christian, I can assure you I wish every multiple I have worked with could be helped by a quick procedure of exorcism. The fact is, it isn't that easy. Patients must undergo a rather lengthy and painful process of reintegration. There are no instant solutions, but by utilizing the tools of prayer and Bible study, the process is much less painful for patients and therapist.

Working with patients with MPD has served to increase my faith in a loving God. It also has served to expose the presence, power, and reality of evil. For it is evil in its purest form that creates the conditions that cause this disorder.

> *It is evil in its purest form that creates the conditions that cause MPD.*

CONCLUSION

Fortunately for all of us, a real and loving God will help those who need help and help those who provide help. The same God who wants the best for all of us gives everyone the ability to choose between the best and something far from it. As long as people have the freedom to choose evil over good, there will be traumatized children who grow up to be very troubled adults. It is hard for some to understand that a loving God would allow evil to exist and permit children and adults to be hurt so badly, but pain and death and evil are a part of the world. Our challenge is to have the proper response to reality.

God created each of us with an extremely powerful instinct to survive. Each person has a mind that can do incredible things when it is traumatized. When a helpless child is victimized and tortured, the mind can split off from the reality that would be too painful to remember. And then, at a time of greater strength, when the horror can be resolved, the survivor can mold the pieces back together into a wonderful whole.

We are fortunate that there is so much potential to heal from the abuse that led to splitting into multiple personalities. The evil that has been inflicted on a helpless child does not have to be reinflicted on the next generation. The prognosis for anyone with MPD is very good with professional help. In the midst of pain and confusion, people with multiple personality disorder can have tremendous hope.

RESOURCES

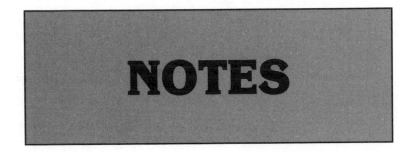

NOTES

Chapter 2

1. Donnel Nunes, "Many Faces of Eve Revealed," *Washington Post,* Sept. 14, 1975, p. A6, col. 4.

2. *Biology of Multiple Personality Investigations,* vol. 1, no. 3/4 (The Institute of Noetic Science, 1985), p. 10.

3. Dr. Colin Ross, *Multiple Personality Disorder: Diagnosis, Clinical Features, and Treatment* (New York: John Wiley and Sons, 1989).

Chapter 3

1. *Diagnostic and Statistical Manual of Mental Disorders,* 3d ed. Revised (Washington, D.C.: American Psychiatric Association, 1987), p. 269.

Chapter 5

1. Brendan O'Regan and Thomas J. Hurley III, "Inner Faces of Multiplicity, Contemporary Look at a Classic Mystery," *Investigations* 1, no. 3/4, (1985): p. 6.

2. Ibid.

3. Brendan O'Regan and Thomas J. Hurley III, "Multiplicity and the Mind-Body Problem," *Investigations* 1, no. 3/4, (1985), pp. 19–20.

Chapter 6

1. Cornelius Wilbur in *Sybil* by Flora Rheta Schreiber (Chicago: Henry Regnery, 1973), and in *The Minds of Billy Milligan* by Daniel Keyes (New York: Random Housc, 1981).

2. James Friesen, Ph.D., *Uncovering the Mystery of MPD* (San Bernardino, Calif.: Here's Life Publishers, 1991), p. 108.

3. Frank W. Putnam, M.D., Juliet J. Guroff, Edward K. Silberman, M.D., Lisa Barban, and Robert M. Post, M.D., "The Clinical Phenomenology of Multiple Personality Disorder: Review of 100 Recent Cases," *Journal of Clinical Psychiatry* 47 (June 1986): p. 288.

4. O'Regan and Hurley, "Inner Faces," p. 3–6.

5. Putnam, Guroff, Silberman, Barban, and Post, "Clinical Phenomenology," p. 288.

6. O'Regan and Hurley, "Inner Faces," p. 5.

Chapter 7

1. Ralph Allison, M.D., *Minds in Many Pieces* (New York: Rawson, Wade, 1980), p. 135.

Chapter 8

1. Brendan O'Regan and Thomas J. Hurley III, "Etiology of Multiple Personality—From Abuse to Alter Personalities," *Investigations* 1, no. 3/4, (1985): p. 11.

2. Friesen, *Uncovering the Mystery of MPD*, pp. 82, 189.

3. Nelly Gupta, "Who Am I?" *Ladies' Home Journal,* March 1990, p. 235; *Journal of Clinical Psychiatry* 47 (June 1986):

290, 292; *Diagnostic and Statistical Manual of Mental Disorders,* 3d ed. (Washington, D.C.: American Psychiatric Association, 1980), p. 271.

4. The four components are taken from O'Regan and Hurley, "Etiology of Multiple Personality," p. 11.

5. James Friesen, Ph.D., "Treatment for Multiple Personality Disorder: Integrating Alter Personalities and Casting Out Evil Spirits," *The Journal of Christian Healing* 11, no. 3 (Fall 1989).

Chapter 10

1. *Time,* Nov. 12, 1990, p. 87.

2. Stephen Buie, M.D., "Introduction to the Diagnosis of Multiple Personality Disorder," *Grand Round Review* (NME Psychiatric Hospital Division), 4th issue, 1992, p. 1.

3. Friesen, *Uncovering the Mystery of MPD,* p. 222.

Chapter 13

1. Friesen, *Uncovering the Mystery of MPD,* p. 72; Larry Kahaner, *Cults That Kill* (New York: Warner Books, 1988), chapters 4 and 5; D. W. Griffin, Ph.D., *Four Faces of Satanism* (1989 unpublished report) pp. 1–17.

2. *Report on Ritual Abuse,* Los Angeles County Commission for Women—Ritual Abuse Task Force, (1991): pp. 4, 10.

3. Kahaner, *Cults That Kill,* p. 20.

Chapter 14

1. Friesen, *Uncovering the Mystery of MPD,* p. 131.

2. Richard Kluft, M.D., "Varieties in Hypnotic Interventions in the Treatment of Multiple Personality," *American Journal of Clinical Hypnosis* vol. 24 (1982): pp. 230–40; Brendan O'Regan and Thomas J. Hurley III, "Signs and Symptoms: How to Recognize MPD," *Investigations* 1, no. 3/4, (1985): p. 16.

Resources

Chapter 15

1. Friesen, *Uncovering the Mystery of MPD,* chapters 5 and 6; Bennett Braun, ed., *The Treatment of Multiple Personality Disorder* (Washington, D.C.: American Psychiatric Press, 1986).

Chapter 18

1. Allison, *Minds in Many Pieces,* p. 83.

2. Allison, *Minds in Many Pieces,* p. 82.

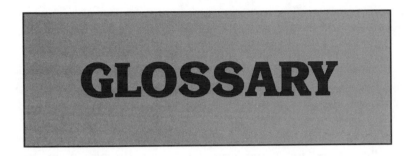

GLOSSARY

Abreaction: The emotional release that results from a remembering or total recall of a past traumatic event that was forgotten because it was too painful.

Alter: An alternate or separate personality that exists within the mind of the patient with multiple personality disorder. The alter is not a separate person but resides in the same body of the person with multiple personality disorder and is a function of the dissociative nature of the disorder.

Coconsciousness: The ability of one alter personality to know the thoughts, feelings, or behavior of another alter.

Copresence: The ability of one alter personality to influence the behavior of another alter.

Core Personality or Birth Personality: The original person who existed before the alter personalities were formed; the name on the birth certificate.

Resources

Dissociation: A defense mechanism that operates unconsciously wherein emotional significance is separated and detached from an idea, situation, or object. In MPD, the ability of the mind to effectively block out the conscious memory and awareness of present events while preoccupied with other thoughts or mental activity.

Egodystonic: Aspects of one's behavior, thoughts, or attitudes that are rejected by the individual as outside one's sense of self.

Egosyntonic: Aspects of one's behavior, thoughts, or attitudes that are viewed as acceptable and consistent with one's sense of self.

Fragment: A fragment personality is a partial alter personality, usually created for a one-time event or a singular purpose or function (e.g., being a "bride").

Fusion: The integration of two or more personalities within one body.

Host Personality: The personality or alter that is in control of the physical body and determines the behavior and actions.

Hypnosis: An altered state of consciousness wherein the individual experiences a state of heightened suggestibility. A tool used in treatment of MPD to rapidly gain access to information not consciously known by the multiple.

Inner Self Helper: A rational alter personality who serves as a memory trace and guide to the therapist. The inner self helper, or ISH, does not otherwise take control of the body except during therapy sessions. Some believe the ISH may be an angelic being or positive spiritual entity; hence, it is not able to be fused like a personality.

Integration: The process of bringing together and blending alters with the result that only one personality exists to respond to outside stimuli. It may start with fusing a few alter personalities or bringing two or more strong alter personalities to coconsciousness or copresence. Ultimately, this process leads to fusion.

Losing Time: For persons with multiple personality disorder, it is the time period during which an alter personality is out and in control of the body, and during the same time, the core personality is amnesiac for what is taking place.

Multiple: A person who has multiple personality disorder.

Persecutor: A negative and primarily self-destructive alter personality in a person with multiple personality disorder; this personality engages in angry, abusive, and violent or destructive behavior.

Rescuer: A resourceful and responsible alternate personality in a person with multiple personality disorder.

Schizophrenia: A mental illness probably caused by a dysfunction in the brain. It is marked by delusions or hallucinations and deterioration in social relationships and self-care. Persons with schizophrenia often "hear voices," but they are not always clearly heard, nor are they personalities. These voices are always heard from a source outside the patient.

Splitting: In multiple personality disorder, the process of dissociation in which an alternate personality is formed.

Switching: The point at which there is an exchange between two alter personalities for control of the body of a patient with multiple personality disorder.

System: The sum of personalities and reactive behavior within a person with multiple personality disorder.

BIBLIOGRAPHY

Beautiful Side of Evil, The. Johanna Michaelson. Eugene, Oreg.: Harvest House, 1982.

Childhood Antecedents of Multiple Personality. Richard Kluft, ed. Washington, D.C.: American Psychiatric Press, 1985.

Courage to Heal Workbook: For Women and Men Survivors of Child Sexual Abuse. Laura Davis. New York: Harper and Row, 1990.

Cults That Kill. Larry Kahaner. New York: Warner Books, 1988.

Diagnosis and Treatment of Multiple Personality Disorder. Frank W. Putnam. New York: Guilford Press, 1989.

Dissociation of a Personality, The. Morton Prince. New York: Oxford University Press, 1978.

Divided Consciousness: Multiple Controls in Human Thought and Action. E. R. Hilgard. New York: Wiley, 1977.

Resources

flock, the (biography of multiple Joan Frances Casey). Joan Frances Casey. New York: Knopf, 1991.

Healing the Incest Wound. Christine Courtois. New York: Norton, 1988.

History of Secret Societies, A. Arkon Daraul. Secaucus, N.J.: Citadel Press, 1987.

I'm Eve (biography of "three faces of Eve"). Chris Sizemore and Ellen Sain Pittillo. New York: Doubleday, 1977.

Katherine It's Time (biography of multiple Kit Castle). Kit Castle and Stephan Bechtel. New York: Harper and Row, 1989.

Man with a Shattered World, The. A. R. Luria. Cambridge: Harvard University Press, 1987.

Michelle Remembers (biography of ritual abuse victim). Michelle Smith and Lawrence Pazder, M.D. New York: Pocket Books, 1983.

Mind of My Own, A (biography of Chris Sizemore—"Eve"—after her final fusion). Chris Costner Sizemore. New York: William Morrow, 1989.

Minds in Many Pieces. Dr. Ralph Allison. New York: Rawson, Wade, 1980.

Minds of Billy Milligan, The. Daniel Keyes. New York: Random House, 1981.

Multiple Man: Explorations in Possession and Multiple Personality. Adam Crabtree. New York: Praeger, 1985.

Multiple Personality. B. Sidis and S. P. Goodhart. New York: Appleton-Century-Crofts, 1905.

Bibliography

Multiple Personality, Allied Disorders, and Hypnosis. Eugene Bliss. New York: Oxford University Press, 1986.

Multiple Personality and the Disintegration of Literary Character. J. Hawthorne. New York: St. Martin's Press, 1983.

"Multiple Personality Disorder and Satanic Ritual Abuse: The Issue of Credibility." Susan Van Benschoten, R.N. *Dissociation* 3, no. 1 (March 1990).

Multiple Personality Disorder: Diagnosis, Clinical Features, and Treatment. Colin Ross, M.D. New York: John Wiley and Sons, 1989.

Multiple Personality: Etiology, Diagnosis, and Treatment. W. N. Confer and B. S. Ables. New York: Human Sciences Press, 1983.

Multiple Personality Disorder from the Inside Out. Barry Cohen, Esther Giller, Lynn W. Baltimore, M.D.: Sidran Press, 1991.

Nightmare (biography of multiple Nancy Lynn Gooch). Lucy Freeman. New York: Richardson and Steirman, 1987.

Nursery Crimes: Sexual Abuse in Day Care. David Finkehor and Linda Meyer Williams with Nanci Burns. Newbury Park: Sage Productions, 1988.

Passion of Adam Bourne, The. M. G. Kenny. Washington, D.C.: Smithsonian Institution Press, 1986.

Prism: Andrea's World. Johnathan Bliss and Eugene Bliss. New York: Stein and Day, 1985.

Resources

Satan's Children: Case Studies in Multiple Personality. Robert S. Mayer. New York: Putnam, 1991.

Satan's Underground. Lauren Stratford. Eugene, Oreg.: Harvest House, 1988.

Split Minds, Split Brains. J. M. Quen. New York: New York University Press, 1986.

Suffer the Child (biography of multiple Jenny Walters Harris). Judith Spencer. New York: Pocket Books, 1989.

Sybil (biography of multiple Sybil Dorsett). Flora Rheta Schreiber. Chicago: Henry Regnery, 1973.

Three Faces of Eve, The (story of treatment for first widely known multiple). Corbett Thigpen and Hervey Cleckley. New York: McGraw-Hill, 1957.

Through Divided Minds. Dr. Robert Mayer. New York: Doubleday, 1988.

Treatment of Multiple Personality Disorder, The. Bennett Braun, ed. Washington, D.C.: American Psychiatric Press, 1986.

Ultimate Evil, The. Maury Terry. Garden City, N.Y.: Dolphin-Doubleday, 1987.

Uncovering the Mystery of MPD. James Friesen, Ph.D. San Bernardino, Calif.: Here's Life, 1991.

United We Stand: A Book for People with Multiple Personalities. Eliana Gil. Walnut Creek, Calif.: Launch Press, 1983.

Bibliography

Victims No Longer. Mike Lew. New York: Nevraumont Publishing, 1988.

When Rabbits Howl. The Troops for Truddi Chase. New York: Dutton, 1987.

Organizations

American Family Foundation
P.O. Box 336
Weston, MA 02193
(617) 893-0931
Deals with education and resources about cults.

Believe the Children
P.O. Box 1358
Manhattan Beach, CA 90266
Deals with children who have been ritually abused.

Center for Dissociative Disorders
College Hospital
10802 College Place
Cerritos, CA 90701

Resources

Child Help USA
6463 Independence Avenue
Woodland Hills, CA 91367
(800) 4-A-Child

Cult Awareness Network National Office
2421 West Pratt Boulevard
Chicago, IL 60645
(312) 267-7777

Cult Project
3460 Stanley Street
Montreal, Quebec H3A 1R8
Canada
(614) 845-64756

DD-Anon Group One
P.O. Box 4078
Appleton, WI 54911
Twelve-Step mutual-help support program for friends and loved ones of those with multiple personality disorder.

F.O.C.U.S.
Families of Crimes of Silence
P.O. Box 2338
Canoga Park, CA 91306
(805) 298-8768
For parents and families of children who have been physically and sexually assaulted; support group in southern California; education and newsletter.

HCA Columbine Psychiatric Center for MPD
8565 South Poplar Way
Littleton, CO 80126

Healing Hearts
1515 Webster Street
Oakland, CA 04612
For survivors of ritual abuse.

Special Resources

International Cult Education Program
P.O. Box 1232, Gracie Station
New York, NY 10028
(212) 439-1550

International Society for the Study of Multiple Personality and
    Dissociation (ISSMP&D)
5700 Old Orchard Road, First Floor
Skokie, IL 60077-1024
(708) 966-4322
Professional organization and newsletter for professionals who
work with multiple personality disorder and includes regional
study groups.

Jewish Family Services Cult Clinic
Jewish Federation Council of Greater Los Angeles
6505 Wilshire Boulevard
Los Angeles, CA 90048
(213) 852-1234

Loved Ones of Multiples (LOOM)
c/o MPD Dignity
P.O. Box 43647
Boulder, CO 80306-4367

Monarch Resources
P.O. Box 1293
Torrance, CA 90505-0293
(213) 373-1958
Books and materials dealing with child abuse—physical, psy-
chological, and spiritual.

MPD Dignity
P.O. Box 4367
Boulder, CO 80306-4367
Self-help organization for those with multiple personality disor-
der.

Resources

National Center for the Treatment of Dissociative Disorders at
  Mount Airy Psychiatric Center
4495 Hale Parkway, Suite 180
Denver, CO 80220
(303) 370-6227
A professional treatment program.

Unbound
P.O. Box 1963
Iowa City, IA 52244
(319) 337-3723
Research and education in multiple personality disorders.

Special Reports, Materials, and Publications

Handbook on Satanism
Center for Christian Education
P.O. Box 5616
Santa Fe, NM 87502
(505) 988-5345

Dissociation
The Journal of the ISSMP&D (see above)
c/o Ridgeview Institute
3995 South Cobb Drive
Smyrna, GA 30080-6397
(800) 345-9775

Heart to Heart, Inc.
2115 Southeast Adams Street
Milwaukie, OR 97222
Books and tapes dealing with child abuse, especially ritual
abuse:
I Can't Talk About It   book, $7.95; tape, $8.95
Don't Make Me Go Back Mommy   book, $7.95—for children
who have been ritually abused in a day-care center

Special Resources

Law Enforcement Primer on Cults
Dale W. Griffis, Ph.D.
P.O. Box 309
Tiffin, OH 44883
Written by a police investigator who has researched satanic and other mind control cults. Send $2.50 to cover postage and handling.

Many Voices
P.O. Box 2639
Cincinnati, OH 45201-2639
Bimonthly publication for those with multiple personality disorder.

MPD Reaching Out
c/o Public Relations
Royal Ottawa Hospital
1145 Carling Avenue
Ottawa, Ontario
Canada K1Z 7K4
A newsletter on multiple personality disorder.

Report on Ritual Abuse
Los Angeles County Commission for Women—
    Ritual Abuse Task Force
383 Hall of Administration
500 West Temple Street
Los Angeles, CA 90012
A $5.00 donation is requested to defray costs.

"Report on the Kern County Child Abuse Investigation"
John Van De Kamp
Office of the Attorney General, Division of Law Enforcement
Bureau of Investigation
State of California; September 1986

Survivorship
3181 Mission Street #139
San Francisco, CA 94110
A publication for survivors and others involved with surviving ritual abuse, torture, and mind control.

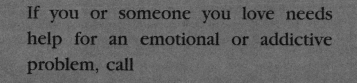